FOUR DAYS AND A YEAR LATER

AN ELEGY

BARRY FRIEDMAN

ZINA —

Thank you for being such a dear friend

Barry

BALKAN PRESS

"I read with an aching heart and more than a couple tears. It's really beautiful. With visceral energy and aching certainty, Barry Friedman writes of a sorrow beyond reckoning, a parent's grief, a father's regret. FOUR DAYS AND A YEAR LATER is compelling, a powerful read, and especially resonant for those of us who have watched a loved one caught away by forces beyond our ability to understand. Wrenching and beautiful and honest, and finally healing in the ways of words and love."

— RILLA ASKEW, AUTHOR *MOST AMERICAN: NOTES FROM A WOUNDED PLACE*

"This is a shattering memoir about love and parenthood and all the ways you can love too much and still lose everything. For anyone struggling to understand the current drug crisis and anyone trying to imagine the outer edges of family this book will both sear and hold you. Powerful, brutally self aware, Barry Friedman is a flashlight through loss and redemption."

— DAHLIA LITHWICK, SENIOR EDITOR, *SLATE*

"Barry Friedman has written a beautiful book of both love and pain where remembrance triumphs over the greatest loss a parent can ever experience."

— JERRY IZENBERG, RED SMITH AWARD FROM THE ASSOCIATED PRESS SPORTS EDITORS, MEMBER NATIONAL SPORTSCASTERS AND SPORTSWRITERS ASSOCIATION HALL OF FAME

"In FOUR DAYS AND A YEAR LATER, Barry Friedman recounts his passage through every parent's worst nightmare—the death of a child. Even more painful, that death happened to Friedman twice—once, slowly, when he lost his son to anger, estrangement, and drugs, and then with shocking suddenness, forever, to a drug overdose. Friedman's courage is exemplary and his voice is true. FOUR DAYS ... is a passage through the hell that millions of families are living during the opioid crisis; it is painful, but important, read . Parents reading this book will want to call their children. I know I did."

— GARRETT EPPS, CONTRIBUTING WRITER, THE ATLANTIC; AUTHOR, *TO AN UNKNOWN GOD: RELIGIOUS FREEDOM ON TRIAL*

"I knew this book would be special after reading the first sentence — 'You died today.' I was right. In FOUR DAYS AND A YEAR LATER, every single word counts. Barry Friedman invites readers to bear witness as he opens his heart and soul and pulls no punches in telling a story of loss and survival that is both tragic and inspirational. This book is simply incredible. What a gift Friedman has created for us."

— MICHAEL WALLIS, AUTHOR, *THE BEST LAND UNDER HEAVEN: THE DONNER PARTY IN THE AGE OF MANIFEST DESTINY*

"This is magnificent. Michelangelo couldn't carve a finer masterpiece. Barry Friedman's FOUR DAYS AND A YEAR LATER is the Pieta of love and heartbreak--a father's devotion to his adored son, his agony over losing him to suicide. A book for the ages."

— SHANE GERICKE, BESTSELLING AUTHOR OF *THE FURY*

"A man walks through the worst days of his life. His son has died. He must confront the biggest questions of all while facing the hundreds of small and seemingly insignificant details of death. But at such a time, everything is significant. Told in sharp shards and jagged pieces that create a riveting and inevitable narrative flow, FOUR DAYS AND A YEAR LATER is brief, powerful, despairing, and yet ultimately, a hopeful expression of what it means to be human."

— WILLIAM MARTIN, *NEW YORK TIMES* BESTSELLING AUTHOR OF *THE LINCOLN LETTER* AND *BOUND FOR GOLD*

"It's a wonderful book. This is a haunting, achingly honest account of an experience every parent fears more than any other—the death of a child. Barry Friedman is a superb writer; this compelling, compulsively readable book will stay with you long after you finish it."

— DAVE BARRY, PULITZER-PRIZE WINNING WRITER

Special thanks to Melissa Moss and Michael Doane. You have both been invaluable to this book and to me.

Four Days and a Year Later

An Elegy

by Barry Friedman

"I can't go on. I'll go on."
Samuel Beckett

1. FRIDAY

YOU DIED TODAY. Maybe you know that.

You are lying on your stomach, inside your mom's house, the house we all lived in together at one time, propped up on your elbows, in your room with three members of the Tulsa Police Department standing over you. I read once, years ago, where the dead are the only ones not surprised by their deaths, but you don't look like you were ready. Your face is full, your cheeks have color. You look asleep. You're on your stomach. It's how you sleep. You're still in your clothes. You could have been drinking last night or fucked up on pot and Adderall and Xanax and methadone before passing out. Interrupted, perhaps, inconvenienced—but not dead.

You're staring at your laptop.

You could still wake up.

You are 24. You *were* 24.

Tense.

That's not a life. It's a number.

But it will have to be.

Twenty-four.

Christmas Eve.

The Tanakh, the Jewish Bible, consists of 24 books.

It's your last number.

YOUR FACE, the more I look at it, though, is more (and less) than full. Your cheeks, bloated, have color, yes, but it's a sick pallor. They are splotchy, too, pockets of red and brown like those found on a sick or an old man. When you slept, when I watched you, you were never propped up like this. You used to lie prostrate, your head buried in the pillow or hanging off the edge of the bed. Your arms outstretched. This pose is off, yet not awful. There's nothing remarkable about seeing you this way. That word, *remarkable*. I'll explain someday, but, no, there's nothing shocking about your body like this: leaden, unresponsive, frozen between tics, lying on the floor with your eyes, still a beautiful but now distant blue, almost rolled back into your head. You get used to the puffiness and hue, a father gets used to it, as well as the labored breathing, the added girth, seeing one's son somewhere inside drugs and despair. I've seen you like this.

This is you.

But you weren't dead.

You were breathing.

I hear walkie-talkies, see cops in latex gloves looking around your room with flashlights. Your mother is in the living room, whispering something to Bob, her husband, your stepfather. Whispering? What are they whispering? Bodies, blue police pant legs keep obscuring my view of you. The cops aren't touching you.

I'm 50, and the only other person I ever saw dead this close was my mother, your grandmother, and she was lying on a king-sized bed in a condominium near Atlantic City and was covered in morphine patches for pain. She was a skeleton, cancer had made a mess of her body, having already eaten away a rib. I was at the foot of the bed, looking at her, her neck and chin taut, her skin olive, her arms at her sides, on her back, partially covered up, her nakedness still that of a young woman. I had never seen my mother naked before. The morphine took the fear out of her, but not the resignation. Death was coming. You could see she knew. She didn't look surprised.

You do.

Your grandmother had metastatic breast cancer; you had drugs. You were not supposed to be the second person I saw dead. I was never supposed to see you dead. You should be the one standing in a doorway with my body, lifeless on the floor or in a bed, and the one wondering what happened and what the cops are doing there and why people are whispering and, later, after the shock passes and the friends and family go home and the food they brought to the house is eaten and my body is buried or cremated, the one who is supposed to be tormented whether you got it right, the two of us, whether you told me you loved me enough, respected me, liked me—whether you did enough. A father is not, I am not, supposed to be the one standing in a hallway mumbling these questions to myself while looking at a dead son who doesn't look dead.

I need to keep your mom out of the room.

"There's nothing good that will come of it," says one of the cops to me.

She's going to want to see you again before … what? The morgue, a gurney, white sheet over your head. What happens next? Remember in *The Godfather*, the first one, after Sonny is shot and Vito Corleone takes the body to Bonasera, the coroner, who owes him a favor, and says, "I don't want his mother to see him this way"?

"Tattaglia's a pimp — he never a could've outfought Santino. But I didn't know until this day that it was — Barzini all along."

You loved saying that line, too, and how Brando stumbled just a little saying it? You did it just like him. You did the stumble. I taught you that. We did it together. I'd give you the cue.

3

"You mean Tattaglia, right?"

I don't want your mom to see you like this.

Your laptop is still on. I can't see the last page you were viewing. What were you looking at? Is that the moment, Paul, that it happened? Is that the moment that will stay with you through eternity, if eternity exists—if you find out it exists so soon after dying and aren't made to wait for either it or the promise of it? Were you buying something, looking at movie times, porn, checking email? *RancidRulz* was your screen name. Had that last page even loaded before your heart imploded or exploded? The last website of your life, what was it? Were you even looking at the screen or were you in the middle of some thought, memory, regret, smile? Did you laugh right before it happened, or was there a sharp pain when you knew it was over, where your life, such as it was, was about to end in your bedroom with you on your stomach on the floor? Did you try to position yourself for a dignified death pose, check your fly, close your mouth? Does death feel like sleep, or like some ooze filling up and choking your body? Does the heart seize up like an engine without oil or does it meander to its end, the beats getting more labored and infrequent? Did the thought, that last one you had, have something to do with that girl in prison to whom you wrote those rambling, grammatically incorrect streams of consciousness in longhand? Her name was Angel, wasn't it, or am I just remembering it that way because you're dead now and I want to believe that was it and angels exist and what a wonderful name for a girl in prison? You wrote about saving her, never stopping for punctuation or a breath. You never mailed any of those letters to her, but you showed them to me. You should have sent them, Paul, all of them, even though they were unfinished and unkempt and preposterous and even though you wouldn't have been able to save her and she would have died anyway and it would have haunted you. They were raw, sweet. They were all you, a language you figured she would understand. And maybe she would have. Was that it? Was your last thought of a girl in jail, an angel in jail? Did you call out for your mom, Taco, me? Did you panic when nobody came?

I can hear you. "Dad, stop asking so many fucking questions. I died. It's over."

I'll stop.

I'm not going to stop.

The cops can't tell me when.

I want to know the time, want to remember what I was doing, where I was standing, what I was thinking. The story, at least from Bob, and even though he's been married to your mother almost twice as long as I (it still doesn't seem right the two of them), is that you were awake this morning around seven, mumbling something incoherent when he told you to get up. Even Taco—Jesus God, your best friend goes by *Taco?*— told Bob he called you at noon and you slurred something, but he couldn't understand what it was. He was in the front yard, drinking from a 2-liter Dr. Pepper when I got to the house, crying, "I'm going to miss him, I'm going to miss him."

I feel like putting that little fuck's head through brick.

So what happened during those last two or three hours, Paul? The television in your room is off, but maybe you played that weird video game on the laptop, the one where you build and destroy cities and then rebuild them again. I remember something about a game set in Newark, New Jersey, a place you called *NEWark*, a place you always wanted to visit.

I am standing in the hallway, down from your room, looking at the cops looking at you, and I see a picture of you with a basketball team in the hallway. You're holding the ball, as if you were the star, as if you were even good at it—as if you even liked the game. You must be 12 or so and you look so normal, happy.

I see myself standing there, a father of a dead son, looking at pictures of my dead son on a wall in a house where I used to live. I can't go on. I'll go on.

I'LL WRITE. What else can I do? What good will it do, can it do? It's my diary, nothing more, and it belongs under the bed, locked up, hidden under some blankets and boxes. I want you to see me write it, though, hear me say it out loud, feel it, help me finish it by nudging me along, letting me know, somehow, in a dream maybe (how trite!), what hurt so much, why this life was so impossible for you, what it was that I never understood about you, or it, or us.

YOU'RE STILL HERE, literally, still here, lying on your stomach. What do you see? Can you see me? I hear that Catholics believe there is a two-hour period between death and when the soul leaves the body—or maybe that's what Jews tell each other about what Catholics believe. Nice notion, though, a two-hour heads up. If you died this morning, and if you were Catholic, you're already gone, but you're not Catholic—you're Jewish. Or I was. Let's go with that. How much time do I have?

YOUR MOTHER and I are not going to agree on a service. I will want Rabbi Sherman to do it at Temple Israel. She will probably want a Methodist service, or I think she will, unless she's found another religion since the last time she found one. In the thirteen years your mother and I were married, each only cared about our faiths when the other did. And now we both will, will both think we should, for some reason that has nothing to do with God or even you. As I said, I'm not sure what faith you had, if any, what you considered yourself the last few years. Your sister, Nina, used to think of herself as Jewish, but ever since the rabbi said in a sermon last year that he wouldn't officiate an interfaith marriage, she's been done.

"That's bullshit," she said, during the service, during the sermon. "It's love. Isn't that all he should be concerned about? We should walk out."

She is an atheist now, convinced the whole notion of everlasting life is silly, a series of fairytales for those unwilling to look deeper.

I'll ask, she'll ask: where was God today?

"WE'RE GOING to have to think about a service, Jane," I tell your mom by the front door.

"You know, he wanted a Viking funeral."

"Huh?"

"Yeah," she said, laughing. "He wanted to be placed on a boat that went out to sea with flaming arrows all around the sides of the boat."

"He did?"

You did?

Where did that come from? And what do you know about the Vikings? I only remember you being on a boat once, now that I think of it, the boat owned by our friends, Ronnie and Louis, who took us out on Grand Lake for the afternoon. You sat with your shirt off, you must have been 12 or 13, and you were thin then and the drugs were at least a year away and you drank Sierra Mist and ate chips. They let you steer the boat. You stood in front of the captain's chair and threw your shoulders back. I should have remembered how good you felt that day, should have catalogued every moment, but I don't. You never mentioned it again, going out on the water, a desire to get back on a boat, and now I hear about Vikings and a sendoff with flaming arrows. Nina tells me you used to watch the History Channel. You liked when Tony Soprano called it The Hitler Channel and maybe there was also programming about Vikings and lost journeys that stayed with you.

THEY JUST PUT you on a gurney and they're trying to maneuver it—you—through the hallway. I don't know where he came from, but a volunteer chaplain from the city is here, too, and he just led us in a prayer and ended it by saying, "In Jesus' name."

Goddammit! I told him when he took out his portable bible that we were from a mixed religious family and not, NOT, to mention Christ's name.

Maybe it's Oklahoma. You should have stayed in Maryland, where you were arrested, and where you'd still be alive if you had. What did you want the cop to do? He sees you asleep, headphones on, in a parking lot, notices a club with spikes coming out of it in the front seat, and a prescription bottle with pills which are clearly not yours. How lucky you were, considering all that, getting off with a fine and unsupervised probation. And then you came back to Oklahoma and back to methadone and Xanax and hydrocodone and that imbecile in the front yard. I wish now they had thrown you in jail in Maryland, kept you for six months, kept you away from all this, kept you away from yourself. I would have preferred visiting you, seeing you dressed in an orange prison suit on a work detail outside of Baltimore than with a sheet over your head on a gurney that's too big for the hallway. Is it true, as your mother told me, that when you were in court in Baltimore, you told your attorney and the district attorney that you would have produced a prescription for the drugs the cop found but that your doctor was in jail for writing illegal prescriptions?

That's hilarious. Did they laugh?

HOW MANY WAYS were there to avoid this Friday afternoon? And how many things had to happen at precisely the moment they did for you to die today? One less drink, one less pill, one more good night's sleep, one dickhead friend who tells you to stop, and maybe your heart holds out and it's a normal Friday and I don't have a dead son.

I CAN'T KEEP the narrative straight, Paul. The stories keep cutting in line. You're lying under this sheet in the hallway. I see the outline of your face, your nose, and I'm trying to remember if the last time we spoke — Wednesday, right, two days ago? — it went all right. You told me you loved me, I remember that. You were on something, clearly, your voice was heavy, yet you were giggling. You told me you loved me and then said you would try to pick me up from the airport. I told you I loved you, but I don't think you heard me. Those were the last words I heard from you. I was in Vegas, at your grandfather's, and the last thing my son, who would be dead before the week was out, said to me was, "I love you."

Maybe it's best if the story ends there. Maybe that's the only story that needs to be told.

I flew back this morning. I didn't expect you to be there. You weren't.

ONE OF THE detectives just pulled me aside and said he found a syringe in your pocket. I can see Taco outside and he's still walking around the front yard, mumbling to himself.

He'll be the next one to die; you know that, don't you?

But today, that little fuck, that little shit gets to go home. He gets to see tomorrow and lie to his parents about needing money for something other than drugs and alcohol. He gets to parlay his grief over you into sympathy and more drugs and sympathy and maybe sex with a girl as fucked up as he will be. He'll use you in death.

The cop who found the syringe told me when he went to ask Taco what happened to you, Taco kept repeating, "I don't know, I don't know. He was my best friend."

This isn't his fault, but I can see him if he doesn't die soon, which he will, at 30 or 35, telling people about his "best friend Paul" and about how he tried to save you but couldn't and I can hear him tell it with earnestness and persuasion and even see the girl who will be with him who will rub his back and cry during his recounting and think to herself, "What an amazing man to have come through all this." And Ryan, yes, by then he'll use his real name, will never mention his sucking on a Dr. Pepper bottle like a tit in the front yard the day you died or how he couldn't put five words together. I want you to be 35, to be able to tell someone, some kid like you, maybe your son, my grandson, about drugs and desperation and survival and have some dark-haired girl by your side, crying and rubbing your back who thinks the world of you.

But you're dead in a hallway. Taco is now getting a ride home.

ABOUT A MONTH AGO, Nina told me how doing drugs was something you enjoyed doing and that your friends looked up to you, that Taco looked up to you.

"I'm tired," she told me, "of Paul always being the victim."

Your sister has always been the smartest one in the family.

ON MY WAY over to your mom's house before, Nina called. I

couldn't talk to her until I stopped moving. I didn't want to be driving when I told my daughter her brother was dead. But then I listened to her message.

"Dad, Dad ... *Dad!*"

Apparently, your mother called her, but was hysterical, couldn't talk, so Bob got on the phone and told her. It wasn't Bob's place to do that. It was mine. It's what fathers are supposed to do.

I imagine Nina was in her dorm at the University of Oklahoma, the dorm used by the athletes, as she would be on any Friday afternoon, when she heard the phone ring. I wonder if there was something about the ring, the moment, that seemed different to her, and then she heard your mother's wail, then Bob's voice.

"Your brother's dead."

And then, Paul, she had to hang up the phone. She had to stand there and figure out what to do next. If there were people in her room, she had to tell them; if not, she had to tell someone, call someone. And what do you do when you hear your brother is dead? Do you close your eyes or open them wide? Do you collapse on the floor where you're standing? Do you understand at that moment the world will never be the same? What do you do when you can't get your father on the phone and your mom's hysterical and your brother's dead?

What do you do when that moment comes?

Her boyfriend, Drew—you remember, Paul?—his brother Garrett died, coming home from some football scrimmage. A number of players had taken their own cars and he was sitting in the back of one of them when, on the highway, someone had the idea to start a paintball fight on an interstate. The windshield of the car Garrett was in got hit, splattering paint, blinding the driver. The car hit a guardrail or another car and somehow Garrett got thrown through and out of the back window. He was killed instantly. Someone had to call and someone in the family had to answer the phone ... answer that call and hear about paintballs and a dead son on the side or in the middle of a highway. The team dedicated the season to him and the coach, a little fat round man, said coaching would never be the same. But it was. They won state, they probably mentioned Garrett during the celebration, but his memory is gone; so, too, are their patches with his number on the uniforms the team wore that year. Drew doesn't talk about it, Nina tells me. I don't know if she'll want to talk about you. You were her big brother, even when you weren't good at it, even when she hated the attention you got. Like your mother, she sometimes called you *Paulie*. It made you sound Italian, made you sound like a small-town hood, what Willi Cicci in *The Godfather* would call a soldier.

Made ... Makes. Tense. I don't know which one to use.

Two dead brothers will be their bond.

ONE OF THE cops just told me they are taking your body to Oklahoma City to do the autopsy because there is no medical examiner's office in Tulsa anymore.

"It usually only takes a day," he tells your mom and me.

"Drugs?" I ask.

He doesn't know, he says. Then, "Yeah, looks that way."

The guy who did the prayer pulls your mom and me aside.

"I'm sorry to say this, but you're going to have to make a decision pretty soon about what to do, what kind of service to have."

"Okay. Give us a minute," I say. "Cremation, I guess. Yeah," I say, I ask. "Sounds like—"

"—Yeah, yeah," she says agreeing, "I think that's what he'd want."

"Where do we do it?" I ask. "For me, you know, I'm more comfortable at Temple Israel. But maybe we can have both."

"No," she says, "Rabbi Sherman was always so good, let's have him do it."

Standing in the hallway, we decided what to do with our dead son. You would have been proud of us.

The thought of you being buried somewhere, somewhere I could go and see you dead, somewhere I would traipse over dirt and other people's dead children—no, that will not happen. I don't want to see you in the ground. I want to take your ashes to The Bahamas or San Diego or some other place you loved, Las Vegas or Columbia, Missouri, maybe even Newark, but not a grave with a headstone and dates and inscription and other people staring at a father who's staring at the ground where his dead son is.

I tell the guy again, "Yeah, cremation."

He tells me there are still arrangements that have to be made and then hands me a card from his funeral home.

"We all work on a rotating schedule. You don't have to use us, but if there's anything I can do, let me know."

I won't be calling.

I FOLLOW YOU OUTSIDE. I touch the back of the van and go back in the house.

How do I tell people you died? Do I mention the drugs? Certainly not the syringe. Or do I just say you're dead?

How do you want people to find out about this?

I SIT in the wicker chair near the fireplace, looking at your mom and your grandmother, her mother, who had driven over before I got there, on the sofa. I notice how your mom is starting to look like her. Bob is on a chair where the blue chair used to be, the one you liked sharing with me when you were younger. You sat in my lap, facing me, your head resting on my thighs. You in pajamas, Dr. Denton's, the ones with the feet, and you were lathered in Baby Magic. I stroked your hair and pulled your feet until your were almost upside down. That's how I knew you were growing. Your legs would inch up my chest. I opened your legs, closed them, played Peekaboo with you. You laughed, I laughed. Your grin, your teeth, your gums — there was nothing more beautiful.

THERE'S a row of laundry over your mom's head and I want it to fall, just so something will happen. I watch Bob dab his eyes. Not one of us knows how to help anyone else. Bob gets up to go to the office, my old office.

I have to call my father to tell him about my son.

Your Aunt Susan just called. I go outside. She's just calling to say hello, it's a coincidence.

"Barry, what is it?"

Sitting on a bench in your front yard, where I can still see the cigarette butts you smoked, I tell her. She promises to call my brother, Wayne, your uncle. I tell her I want to tell our father. She says she's coming to Tulsa for the service.

"There may not be one."

"I'm coming," she insists.

MY WIFE SUSAN, your stepmother, called. She's on her way.

We've been married five years, Paul, and you only saw her three times, the last just a month ago.

She never got over you not coming to our wedding.

WHEN I COME BACK INSIDE, I go to your room, where Jill and Marcia, your mom's cousins, are cleaning up your death.

"Don't let Jane come in here," Marcia says. "I mean it. Don't let her come in here."

She walks by me, carrying rags, towels. They're wet, there's blood. It's your blood. Why is there blood? I see her walk through the living room. I follow her and see her look at your mom, smile, without breaking stride, and disappear into the laundry room. I sit again in the wicker chair.

EVER SINCE YOUR mom and I divorced, and that's now 16 years, I have never been comfortable coming back to this house. What was the name of that girl who you used to date, not the one in prison, the other one who told me that what bothered you most about the divorce was not that I moved out or that Bob moved in or that your mom married him, but that nobody asked you what you thought, nobody ever gave you the chance to be the man of the house?

You were eight. Did you really tell her that? Did you want that?

FOR MY BIRTHDAY ONE YEAR, Nina gave me a picture. I am lying on my back; she is sitting on my stomach, she must have been two or three, wearing a purple hat, looking back at the camera.

"Dad," she told me, "it's the only picture I have of you when I was little."

"You look adorable," I said.

"Why aren't you happier?"

Looking at it now, and I have it in my bedroom, I can see she's right. I wasn't happy back then. You weren't, either, were you? I wonder if our unhappiness, mine and yours, was linked, our shared inability to get easy moments right. Where are the pictures of us, Paul, the two of us? Do you have them?

· · ·

THE WICKER CHAIR IS UNCOMFORTABLE; I move to its ottoman. It's worse. In Judaism, when someone dies, the mourners sit shiva and sit on hard chairs. I am sitting shiva in my old house for my son who's on a gurney in the back of a van that by now is getting on Interstate 44 for the 90-mile drive from Tulsa to Oklahoma City.

I can't remember the last good memory you and I had in this house. I keep looking at the laundry on top of the sofa. Your grandmother is about finished folding the remainder of the towels.

It could be any other Friday afternoon if you didn't know better.

YOU LOVED THIS HOUSE, didn't you? When your mom's dad died, you said you saw his spirit outside your bedroom window. Your mom told me she had walked into your room, you must have been seven, and you were sitting in a chair, looking outside, when she asked, "What are you doing?"

"Talking to grandpa."

Are you out there now, by your window? Can you see Marcia and Jill in your room, cleaning up? Do you want to talk to someone?

I DON'T KNOW how long to stay here. Your grandmother is asking questions about laundry and dinner and your mom is answering her. Her daughter, your mother, does not need small talk; she needs wisdom, warmth, a mother. I remember something an old girlfriend—you remember Claudia, from Germany, don't you?—told me when her dad died. "I wanted," she said, "a mom with big breasts and I wanted her to hold me. I want be buried in breasts and cleavage. But my mom's not that mom, she doesn't have those breasts, doesn't know how to hold me."

• • •

BOB KEEPS ALTERNATING between his office and his chair where ours used to be. He doesn't sit by your mom, doesn't come over to hold her hand.

SUSAN, your stepmom, just arrived, and your mother goes to meet her at the door.

"I can still feel Paul in the house," Susan, who has never been here, says, hugging her. I am watching these two women embrace because my son is dead. You are bringing an ex-wife and soon-to-be ex-wife together.

YOUR MOM and I had a fight about a year before we got divorced. We were in the kitchen, screaming at one another, and you came in, threw your hands between us like a ref stopping a fight, and screamed, "Enough, enough. No more."

Eight-year-olds shouldn't have to break up fights between parents. They should wear pajamas with feet and fall asleep in their dad's lap in a blue chair from Sears as their legs grow up his chest. And your mother and I were better afterward ... for a while. You did that. I'm sorry for putting you through that. Three months after your mom and I divorced, I moved to North Hollywood, California and wound up living in a loft that I rented from a comedian friend. It was miserable, my lost year in Los Angeles, for a lot of reasons, guilt mostly for leaving you and your sister. One morning around 6:00, the phone rang. It was you. You were headed to school.

"Just want you to know, dad, when you moved out there, I cried. I have to go now."

Eight-year-olds shouldn't have to do that, either.

• • •

THEY'RE STILL HUGGING. When Susan and I moved into our house, your mom came over with salt and bread, an old Jewish custom for good luck and a happy life and home. When she left, Susan tossed them both in the trash.

"Why did you do that?" I asked.

"I didn't marry your old life."

Watching them now, I see how little in common I have with either. Neither thinks I am (or was) a good father. Susan feels I did you much harm, telling me a number of times how much you hated my first book, *Road Comic*, especially the parts where I wrote about the time I hit you and the time you pulled the knife on me. She thought I manipulated stories to make myself look like the adoring, concerned father when, in reality, I was absent, inconsistent, judgmental, and doing it all for show. She thought when I wasn't being cruel or exploitive, I was trafficking in cheap sentiment. And what of the part, I asked, about sitting outside Mario's Pizzeria, where you worked, just so I could see you smile?

"He was a prop to you."

Did you think so? Did you even read it?

THEY'RE HOLDING EACH OTHER, crying.

RABBI SHERMAN JUST CALLED BACK. He's in Iowa, but he'll be back tomorrow or Sunday night and, of course, he'll do the service.

Okay with you?

"What happened, Barry?"

"Drugs," I tell him.

I hear him exhale.

. . .

SUSAN NEEDS TO GO. She was supposed to be singing in Dallas this weekend and was just about to leave when Bob called to tell me about you. I thought about not telling her.

I walk her outside.

"Can I do anything?" she asks.

"I'm glad you're here."

"Where else would I be?"

We don't hug.

YOUR MOM IS TIRED. It's about six thirty. I have been here more than three hours. The rabbi called again and gave me the name of a funeral home that handles the deaths of Jews in town. I have to call them tomorrow.

YOUR GRANDFATHER JUST CALLED, as I was leaving the house. I let it go to voicemail. I check. He has won eleven hundred dollars at craps at the Red Rock Casino by pressing his bets he tells me.

"I could have made more," he says.

He's 81. Once on a courtesy van to the airport, I heard two guys talking and the conversation went like this:

Man 1: You hear about Bill's mom?

Man 2: No, what happened?

Man 1: She died.

Man 2: Oooh, sorry. How old?

Man 1: 95

Man 2: 95? Well, that's enough.

Your grandfather loves that story. He has outlived his grandson. Whenever he tells me stories about friends of his who have died late in life, he'll say something like, "Lived to ninety. Did all right." Even when talking about your grandmother, when she died at 69, and even though he maintains she could have, should have, had ten more years, will say, "She wasn't cut short. She had a life." Did you have a life? You didn't, did you? Your mother once showed me your plans and goals that you had written on a folded-up piece of graph paper. You had each year, 2004, 05, 06, clearly marked. You wanted to open a restaurant, one of the items said. You wanted to design software, another entry. You wanted to be a professional skateboarder. You stopped making entries after 23.

I AM IN THE CAR, driving down Harvard Avenue, toward my own home. There are memories but it's raining, so I don't trust them. I pass Mario's, closed but lit up. It was our lighthouse. You were thirteen when you first started working there—right here—but I can't seem to remember why I thought this was a good idea. It was where you got your first paycheck. It was where you first got high.

IT'S FRIDAY. It was our "Pizza Night," remember? When you and Nina were little we made sure we did something special each day I had visitation. Monday was the night we made spaghetti and monster meatballs or shrimp in a cheap T-fal pan; Tuesday, we went to buy candy at Mr. Bulky's; Wednesday, we had bagels; Thursday, we went to the arcade at the mall after dinner; and Friday, we came to Mario's and had pizza. When Nina was little and could barely look over the counter, they'd give her dough to play with; Saturday ... what was Saturday, anyway?; and Sunday, we went driving around Tulsa, stopping for ice cream or cheap burgers. We saw the same sights and you and Nina took turns sitting in the front seat of my white Mazda GLC. I'd charge you both a dime if either one of you failed to put on your seatbelt within ten seconds of starting the car. I never collected, did I?

You owe me money.

YOUR GRANDFATHER JUST CALLED AGAIN. He doesn't trust answering machines, he said in his message, just calling again to tell me about his day and his big win. He also played tennis, went to the gym. The casino comped him at the buffet. His life is perfect.

I'M HOME NOW. Florence Avenue. Your grandmother's name. It was a house you saw only a few times. We sat on the porch once one day and had snacks, after I ran into you at a strip center, across from the University of Tulsa. There was a Burger King, a place that made keys, a pawn shop, and a laundromat. You were leaning against your white Jeep, drinking a soda.

"What are you doing?" I asked, crossing the street. I was on a walk.

"Just hanging out."

"Here? Why here?"

"Just am. You live around here, right?" you asked.

"Yeah, wanna come over?"

"Okay, sure. I guess."

WHEN SUSAN and I bought the house, I thought living on a street with the name Florence would be beautiful, quixotic, poetic, and serendipitous. It's just dark now and the house foreign when I walk in. There are no connections—or maybe too many. I was supposed to have dinner tonight with Rick, who used to own that restaurant with the great bread you used to love. I called to apologize for not letting him know sooner, but for the first time to a non-family member, I had to say the words, "My son died."

"I'm sorry, buddy." He said he'd make something special for

your service because he's a chef and that's what he does.

I'M IN THE HOUSE, sitting at the kitchen counter, running my fingers along the grout, and your Uncle Wayne just called. He doesn't know what to say. Hope, his wife, doesn't either. They're coming to the service. I told them what I told your aunt.

Jews bury their dead within 24 hours, unless it falls on the Sabbath, which just started, so Sunday is the earliest day for the service, which won't happen. You may not come back from Oklahoma City—your remains, your ashes in a box—until Monday, so that will be the earliest.

I CALLED MY AGENT, Kevin, in Las Vegas, to tell him and to talk about upcoming gigs he had scheduled for me. After your grandmother died, he called and said, "Whenever you want to work again, let me know. Any week. It's yours." I am supposed to work in Providence next week and then Vegas three weeks after that.

"You want me to cancel them?" he asks.

"I don't know. Let's wait."

YOUR GRANDFATHER IS LISTENING to the stereo in his office when I call. The volume is loud enough for me to hear.

"Dad, turn off the stereo."

"Okay, okay, what?"

"Dad, please."

Nothing.

"Dad, please. Turn the fucking thing off."

He does.

"What is it, sweetheart?" He sometimes calls me that.

"What's the matter?"

No sound comes out of my mouth.

"Barry, what?"

"Paul ..." I can't finish it.

"Barry, what is it?"

I keep trying; I keep getting stuck. Then "... died tonight."
It came out.

"What? What happened?" he asks.

"I think it's drugs. Doesn't matter."

"Oh my God," he said. "Oh my God." And then, "Oh,
Barry."

I THINK he tells me it will be all right, asks if I need anything,
but I don't hear or feel anything because my back is spasming.
Paul, I can hear the spasms.

"I'll call you back, dad."

"You okay?"

"Yeah."

YOUR UNCLE WAYNE calls again and is wondering how Price-
line works — especially when it comes to hotels. We talked about
hotels, we did. It was strangely soothing.

I see Aunt Susan is trying to call. I click over.

"Did Wayne just call you about the hotel? I told him not to
bother you."

Family. It doesn't stop.

She is something, my sister, your aunt. I love her more the
older I get. At times she reminds me of my mother, your
grandmother.

"Mom's not going to be happy," she said. "She's waiting for
Paul, you know."

"Yeah, I know. Claudia once said that Mom was on a white

puffy cloud throwing down thunderbolts to burn the asses of the people she hated."

"Paul will enjoy helping her."

"Yeah."

"Either of them ever meet Claudia?"

"No."

"I think they both would have liked her, Barry. You going to call her?"

"Someday."

MY EYES STING. I feel like I've been punched in both of them.

I'LL WRITE MORE TOMORROW, but I'm going to bed now. I'd wait up for Susan, my wife, but I don't want to be disappointed. You never thought of her as your stepmom; she never thought of you as her stepson. My life, my children, were not her life; I'm not sure I was her life, either.

I REMEMBER ONCE when your Uncle Wayne and I were younger, sixteen and fourteen — he's older — and we were out late one night. Your grandmother started worrying. We didn't have a curfew, something she and your grandfather never imposed, but for some reason this night, she had a bad feeling, a premonition. This was before cell phones, so there was nobody to call, no texts to send.

"Barry," she told me later, "I was beside myself."

She didn't wake up your grandfather, which she thought of doing. Instead, she said she paced through our rooms, through the kitchen, even the garage, until she got tired, very tired, and couldn't stay awake any longer, so, to hear her tell it, she looked up to the ceiling and said to God, "You better be up there, because I'm going to bed." It's a wonderful image: your grandmother, standing in a housecoat, looking up at the ceiling in the middle of her living room, pointing a finger at God and demanding, not asking, *demanding*, he make sure her children were safe.

That story has nothing to do with you.

That story has everything to do with you.

2. SATURDAY

I DID SLEEP. Not straight through, which wouldn't have happened even if you hadn't died.

I saw the clock at 2:12 a.m. and then again at 6:23 a.m. That's four hours and eleven minutes. I'll take that any night. The night after my son dies, I feel guilty about sleeping so well. What kind of father can sleep? I had chills as I got into bed, accompanied by a headache and nausea and a sharp pain over my right eye, but had I not reminded myself that you were dead, I could have convinced myself it was something else — something I ate, a sinus problem, a migraine. It would have been just another bad night's sleep and not the worst one at that. You were two or three, lying on the floor on your stomach in your grandmother's house, using a yellow crayon on Curious George. You were leaning on your elbows, staring down, so focused, so peacefully alive. So unremarkably remarkable.

I used to think of this before you were dead, too.

I CALLED the funeral home last night, before going to bed. I could have left a message, but imagined someone having to hear it, some employee coming into work, after putting down her coffee and paper and donut, hitting PLAY. How many frantic, incoherent messages does the home get from some sobbing family member who tells of a mother's, father's, daughter's, or son's death? How many times does she have to replay the message so she can get past the screams and sobs and panic to retrieve the name of the dead, the survivors, the phone numbers so she can call back? I am lying here, looking at the ceiling, and see the same cracks, one in particular that runs at an angle from the southeast to the northwest that I see every morning, thinking about that woman—I don't know why I know it's a woman—who would have had to hear my message about your death.

There's no reason the ceiling should cave in, but if it did, today, right now, I wouldn't move to get out of the way. I wouldn't cover up. Let them find me in a bed under a blanket of sheetrock and asbestos and insulation.

I am paralyzed. Still, underneath a ceiling that I am imploring to crash on my head, I decide—yes, I decided right then and there— to be a better father in death to you than I was in life. I am going to get through this weekend without falling apart, at least not in public. I will not be the father who needs help up the stairs, or wails in a synagogue, or leaves incomprehensible, wretched messages on the answering machines of funeral homes that are particularly sensitive to dead Jews. I will throw my shoulders back. This is how a father grieves. The ceiling has varicose veins, and Fitzgerald's, a very Irish-sounding name, its sensitivity to us notwithstanding, doesn't open for an hour. I'm not calling, even though I could make sense, talk calmly. I will go over there. I get out of bed, walk around the house, stopping in odd places, between the hallway and kitchen, and lean against the wall that looks out to the dining room. I walk back to the bedroom and see Susan, sleeping. I forgot to mention she came home. I think about getting back into bed. I don't. Instead, I go upstairs to my office and check email, to read the news. The world woke up, too. It goes on.

FOR THE SECOND time since you died, I doubled over in excruciating pain. It happened last night in bed, but this morning, I was sitting on the toilet and it felt like my breathing, my blood flow, everything else just stopped. Even the sob, which I felt coming, didn't come. I was a screaming baby in the moment between wails, the eerie moment between them when nothing happens. Last night, I rolled over on my side and curled my knees thinking it would put less pressure on my heart. This seizure, if that's what it was, didn't last long, perhaps a few seconds, but my heart literally felt like it was going to explode, which is what may have happened to yours, and I could sense the fluid and the blood, the tissue splattering against my inner chest. Sitting on the toilet, just before, trying to fit my foot in the tile square without going over the grout to the next tile, it happened again, but even more painful this time. It felt like a cancerous mass in my bowel had just metastasized and was coursing through my gastrointestinal tract. It felt like water running down my leg, only internally. I could feel the poison. I thought last night in bed, I thought just before on the toilet, a father cannot die the same day as his son. No God is that much of a motherfucker. I cannot die on the toilet. Elvis did.

I took a shower, brushed my teeth, put on generic minoxidil. You're dead less than a day and I still care if I go bald. I got dressed. I got dressed yesterday. It's a miserable day at the moment. It's still raining. I drive to Fitzgerald's. I feel like I'm in slow motion but everything else is at normal speed. Before I left, Susan asked if I wanted her to go. Why does she keep asking me what she should do?

"No, it's okay."

There's not a car in the parking lot when I pull in. The rain is really coming down. It rained this kind of rain the day your grandmother died. It's a little after 8:00, and the place looks empty. Maybe I'll just sit here. I can't just sit here. I try the side door. It's open. The furniture inside looks like something out of a grown-up dollhouse. Some of the chairs have doilies on their backs and the end tables and chests look almost miniature. The rooms are empty, small, musty, something out of *Arsenic and Old Lace*. It's brittle in here.

"Hello," I call out. "Hello."

A man comes out from an office.

"Can I help you?" he says.

I immediately like his smile, demeanor.

"I'm Scott."

It's not a woman. So much for that.

"My son died. I don't have an appointment."

He ushers me into one of the offices.

"I'm from Temple Israel."

"The owner will want to know," he says, and picks up the phone and calls someone. He hangs up. "That was David Dopp. He's the owner. He wants to know when someone from the temple is here. Do you want anything?"

"Diet Coke."

He returns, gives me the can.

"I'll be down the hall. Take the time you need. I have some things I have to do."

I sit in this office, looking at fax machines, pictures of people who, I assume, are the owners. There are no pictures of the dead. Of course there aren't. The Diet Coke tastes like metal. Is it possible it always does?

Scott comes back with a folder.

"Do you need more time?" he says.

"No. I need to bury my son," I say, more dramatically than I intend.

"I'm sorry. I'll do everything I can. You want another Diet Coke?"

"Yeah."

I need to bury my son.

The shovels, the dirt, the coffin, the other headstones, the gravediggers and green tarps, the folding chairs where your grandfather and grandmother will sit, maybe the wind and rain that will be blowing and falling—they're all metaphors. I'm not burying you. I'm cremating you. The distinction in death. It's soothing right now. I'm going to sprinkle you in the Atlantic I've decided, as you wish, and hope the Vikings with fanfare come get you, take you in, make you one of their own, and take you where you want to go. Your way is better.

As SCOTT WAS FILLING out the folder and the forms inside—his writing is meticulous and he appears to be writing in all caps but the words he writes are not shouting—he asked about your profession. I didn't want to tell him you didn't have one, didn't want to say you were in charge of the ovens at Mario's, making sure the pizzas weren't over or undercooked, didn't think you'd want to be known as a wardrobe assistant, even though that was the last job you had in Oklahoma City when you worked crew on that horror movie that your mom was costuming. But then I remembered about that list you carried around. There was a line drawing, too, wasn't there? Intricate lines and boxes and ghoulish figures inside those boxes. It wasn't on you when you died and you usually carried it around with you. Where is it?

"He was an artist."

He writes it down.

Artist.

Good. The world, those who read this obituary and wonder about Paul Friedman, will read that you were an artist. Scott asks whether your mother and I have come to any decision about burial.

"We have," I tell him, "but let me call her just to be sure."

"JANE, SORRY TO ASK YOU THIS," using Scott's phone, "but I'm here at the funeral home. I can't believe we have to talk about this again, but cremation, right?"

"Yeah, I think. Yes. You?"

"Yes, I think so, too."

I tell Scott and he checks a box.

You're going to be cremated after you come back from Oklahoma City, after an autopsy is done, a standard procedure, apparently, when someone dies somewhere other than a hospital. In your case, since the assumption is that drugs killed you, there will also be a toxicology report. Scott tells me after the autopsy is done, someone from the coroner's office, or Fitzgerald's, will drive you back to Tulsa. Your ashes will be in a box or an urn, and then someone from the funeral home will bring you to the sanctuary at Temple Israel for the service.

The service is going to be Monday, as long as the rabbi comes back from Iowa in time, as long as you come back in time. There's a backlog of autopsies to be done in Oklahoma City. If you're not here, the service will not happen until Tuesday, your mom's birthday.

"There was no foul play," Scott tells me, "so he should. But it's possible, okay?"

"How do you know ... about the foul play?"

"It would have said so here," he says, opening the folder that he's been working on and indicating the paperwork inside.

"You already have ..."—I don't even know what I'm asking —" ... the police report?"

"Yeah," he says.

No foul play? Drugs and a syringe are not considered foul play?

Monday is good. I actually thought those words — "Monday is good" — as it will also allow your grandfather, aunt, and uncle to get here. Aunt Susan and Uncle Wayne called this morning to say they wish they had done more for you. When your grandfather called, he wanted to talk about flights and hotel reservations. You never came up.

IT WILL COST $1,608 to have you cremated and that's without a funeral procession — limos, flowers, attendants, which would add another $2,200. Had we buried you, probably twice that. There's a Friedman family plot in Long Island, where your grandmother is and where you could be put to rest for free, which would save us some money. But we'd still have to get there, hire a rabbi (there are rabbis just walking around the cemetery for just these occasions), and a limo and a stone and I don't know what else. It's the one tangible benefit to being part of the family circle: a free place to be buried. For years, your grandfather would tell me, "You know what a plot costs these days? It's not cheap, baby." All the Friedmans are buried there. When your grandmother died, she left word she wanted her headstone to be mauve. I called the family circle president, a woman named Ida, to tell her I was getting a pink stone.

"You cannot," Ida said. "Family circle rules."

"What?"

"Yes, they must be gray. They're in the bylaws."

"There are bylaws about the color of headstones?"

"Yes, there are!"

Fuck Ida.

The monument company near the cemetery didn't make them in pink anyway.

When your grandmother was alive, she paid the family

circle dues for all of us, something your grandfather does now. He doesn't talk much about his own death, but when he does, he always says, "Whatever happens, you get me back there, next to your mother." There's a plot reserved for him, in fact, right next to her, and also near his mother and father. There's a woman named Betty Koralchek, someone nobody in the family seems to know, on the other side of your grandmother. Your great uncle Hi, your grandfather's brother, has the following engraved on his headstone: "Why make things easy when, with a little work, you can make them difficult?"

You won't be there.

Scott asks again if we want limousines, ushers?

"Some people find it easier," he says.

"No, I don't think so."

What do you think, Paul? You want limos and ushers? The people who are left, Paul, those with recently dead sons in Oklahoma City morgues have to make these decisions on rainy Saturday mornings in front of a sweet man with meticulous handwriting.

I see a candy dish filled with mints and chocolates, a phone on a credenza, and that file with your name on it. My son is dead and I know it's true because there's a file on a desk in a funeral home that proves it. It's not a dream.

But nothing feels real.

Before leaving, Scott tells me about the obituary announcement, which he promises to write, and gives me his cell number and tells me to call anytime. I get up to leave. I am accomplishing things this morning. I am being that father. There's strength in that.

Bullshit.

Not bullshit.

I tell Scott again we definitely—What is this? The third time now?— won't need the procession or the limos or the attendants.

"I'm going to come anyway," he says. "I'll bring Paul and make sure everything runs smoothly. I'm not charging you."

"Thank you. Why?"

"I just want to."

Scott picks up the house phone to call someone. I can't make out what he's saying.

"That was Mr. Dopp again. He sends his condolences. He wants to know when the service will be. And he'll be there on Monday, as well."

"That's nice. What else do we need to go over now?"

"Nothing right now."

My eyes are stinging. I say goodbye, walk out to the car and remind myself, again, to stand up straight. I throw my shoulders back. Yes, this is how I'm going to do it.

ON THE WAY HOME, I stop at Panera to get bagels, but mostly just to stop. When I get home, Didi, Susan's friend, is there and has already brought a box of bagels from Panera as well. She hugs me.

"I brought bagels, too," she says, laughing, crying.

There was much about my life, my friends, you didn't know. Didi and Susan used to get together on Sunday mornings and write. She's a poet; Susan is a songwriter. They would get together, first get high, and then go for coffee, and then, if there was any time left, actually work.

There are twenty-six Panera bagels on the kitchen counter and three people in the house.

EVEN WHEN YOU and I weren't talking to each other during that year and a half, after I found out about you and the drugs, after I gave you an ultimatum, which I thought for sure I couldn't lose (which I did), I talked about you to people like

Didi. You do remember, I hope, that you and I were as close, maybe closer, than I am now with your sister. Back when you were 11, 12, 13, there was no father and son like us. I remember telling a friend of mine, a good comedian friend back then, about something Nina did, and he asked, "You have a daughter? You never talk about her. I thought it was just Paul."

Just Paul.

Back then, it was. I think it hurt Nina, too, though I never thought about that. I also didn't think being a father was tough. Having a son, having you for a son, was easy, effortless. There was a time, after you and I made up, your sister called me, crying.

"What is it, sweetie?"

She didn't know how to tell me. She didn't want to tell me.

"I'm afraid that now that you and Paul are talking, you're going to forget about me."

"That's crazy. That would never happen. Don't be ridiculous."

Your sister was in pain and I dismissed it. Sound familiar? That moment wasn't mine to dismiss.

I want to confess something to you, want to go back to something. I was wrong to stop talking to you. I'm telling you now. But the drugs and your insistence on that drive to school that day to do them, broke me in half. I thought if you had to make a choice between drugs and your father, especially a father whom you seemed to love and admire, especially a father who was as close as I was to you, it would be easy. You'd pick me.

You didn't.

But that wasn't the moment, was it, the one that stomped out everything you and I had? It was another one, another drive to school, another discussion about drugs and lying, only this time you were in 9th grade. You were 14.

"Paul, this has to stop."

"Why?"

"How about because it's wrong and it's dangerous? How about because it's killing your mother? How about because I'm your father and I am telling you to?"

And you laughed.

"You're not a real father," you said. "Why don't you just go back on the road and fuck girls and stop pretending that you're in my life. Go fuck yourself."

And that's when, a little after three in the afternoon, on Harvard Avenue, between 81st and 91st, near a cemetery and your old elementary school, I reached across the front seat and became the kind of father who hits his son in the face with an open palm.

You remember? Of course you remember.

It was after that, days, weeks after, after you and I stopped talking, after I realized there was no more you and me, that there was no more son, that I decided Nina and I would be different. And it was. It was easier because—who knows why? —different DNA, chemistry? My daughter would never tell me to go fuck myself; I'd never hit her. We'd never give each other a reason to. But I didn't get closer with her to show you up. I always imagined you thought that. But I did it to show you that I could be a father, a good one. I wanted you to see me be that kind of father. That's why I kept coming into Mario's. I wanted to stay in your life, even if it meant not talking, even if it meant looking at people as they looked at us looking at each other. I wanted to see you, check on you. All the times I was there were all the times I wanted to come across the counter and hug you, kiss you, apologize, say something smart or profound or funny or new to make all those moments I disappointed you go away. I came in to the restaurant, too, thinking you might want to say something, that you might take the opportunity to start us again. I know people looked at me and said, "What kind of father doesn't talk to his son? What kind comes to his place of work to torture him like this? What kind of bastard does this?" I thought if you saw me, saw me as a father to Nina, you would want it, me, again and that something would click inside you and you would remember the two of us whole. I wanted you to come across the counter and join us at a table, make fun of my hair, bring dough from the back and plop it down on the table so Nina could play with it again as she used to.

How many nights did I eat there with Nina, with others, that you and I didn't talk? Silence. You stealing glances at me, me stealing them at you. What was I thinking? What were you thinking? Our only means of communication was when you tapped the bottom of the tray to let me know it was hot, something you did for every customer, and my nodding that I understood.

As I DRIVE out to your mom's with one of the boxes of bagels, I think of that choreography. Father and son, ten feet apart, separated by a cash register and pastries in a glass container. I could have made it better.

I pull into the driveway, park next to your Jeep. Before going inside, I walk to the other side of the house to where your room is. I peer in the window, holding bagels. Is this where your grandfather stood when you talked to him? I'm here. Talk to me. I go around to the front door. Your mom lets me in.

"Where's Bob?"

"He's out, looking for answers he said."

"What do you mean 'answers'? To what?"

"He's looking for Paul's murderer."

"What?"

Bob is certain you couldn't have done this to yourself, that someone must have shot you full of whatever that syringe in your pocket was filled with, so, apparently, he's been scouring the neighborhood, going to your friends' houses, looking for clues, looking for who killed you.

"He is convinced," she told me.

"Of what?"

"Something to do with some girl at the Texaco station who was supposedly with Paul Thursday night."

As your mother was telling me this, I realized we were standing in the same place in the kitchen, the same proximity to one another that we stood when you tried to get us to stop arguing all those years ago.

"You know—"

"I know," she said, I suppose anticipating my reaction. "But it's how he's dealing with his grief."

She's right.

WHEN BOB GETS BACK, he says that the girl at the Texaco station told him that you never liked shooting yourself up, so you always had people do it for you, but that she wasn't with you last night and she doesn't know who was. He said he's going out again soon to follow more leads.

Leads?

Bob was a cop, right, a long time ago in New York City, before he came to Tulsa to sell insurance. I met him at the comedy club in Tulsa before your mother did. He used to sit in the front row and the comedians used to torture him, something he never seemed to mind. He liked comedians, he liked me, more actually than your mother did towards the end of our marriage. I think they met at some Boy Scout function. I was out of town, doing comedy, and he was there helping out the scout leaders when your mom and you showed up. I found some pictures of the two of them. He was wearing a toupee then and your mom, like every woman in my life when my relationship with them was about to end, looked great and sexy and full of life. We were driving on 81st, near your house, when she told me about him. Don Henley's "The Last Worthless Evening" came on and she started singing along—singing, to me, I guess. "This is the last worthless evening that you'll have to spend"—and then whispered to herself, "Is that ever true."

SO THE SYRINGE in your pocket, Paul, what was that? How many other times did you shoot up before last night and beat death? And how come last night was different? Was there nobody to kick you hard enough to wake you? How many times did something else prevent your heart from doing what it did, or failed to do, yesterday? Was it as simple as a phone ringing or someone dropping a glass or you just having to get up to pee that saved your life?

KRISTIN JUST CAME BY, carrying a car seat, and a baby boy.

Yours?

Your mother said Kristin told her months ago it was. Your mom also said you denied it, said it was some Mexican kid's, and that the baby doesn't even look like you. I don't have the strength to look for myself, to meet my grandson, if it's my grandson, especially not today.

I remember the first time I met Kristin. You brought her with you to dinner at On the Border. You told me she was an opera singer. You were so proud of what she did, which I thought strange. Not that you were proud, but that this girl across the table with a bowl of chips in front of her, which she ate with both hands, rhythmically, first one hand, then the other, chip between her fingers, was actually an opera singer. When she went to the restroom, you said she was living on the street and was "a little fucked up."

I got the unmistakable sense this homeless opera singer was purging.

"She's nice, though," I said.

"You like her?" you asked.

"If you're happy, I'm happy."

I didn't know what else to say.

She doesn't seem to remember me now, certainly doesn't know I want her and a baby who may be my grandson out of your mother's house. Your mom is standing over the car seat and is smiling.

People are coming by the house, some I know, some I don't, and Kristin hasn't moved. Your mom comes in to the kitchen to tell me Kristin came as soon as she heard the news about you.

"She has nowhere to go," she says.

"What are you going to do?" I ask. "Let her stay?"

"I don't know."

I find the wicker chair.

Some of your friends are here. There's an exaggerated torpor to them, a perfected sloth. None of them look like this is the first time they stopped to pay respects to a dead friend who was found with a syringe in his pocket.

Your mom, I can tell, is gaining strength from the people who are here, even your friends. Her house has life, energy, and her smile is unforced. When I walked in this morning, I hugged her again. In all the years we've been divorced, all physical contact between us was minimal and self-conscious, as it probably should have been, but your death makes it easier for me to embrace her. It's not sexual, not even really tender. It's history and guilt. Two parents who will be constant reminders to each other of how they failed their son.

YOUR FRIEND KATIE just stopped by. She's drunk, it's not even noon, and with some guy in a thin tie and a stupid hat. I met her in the doorway between the living room and kitchen.

"Remember me?" she asks.

"Of course," I say, "you were the one who told me about Paul wanting to be the man of the house. I remember the conversation."

"That was me, yeah. When's the service? I'm going to be there," she says before starting to cry.

"Monday, I hope. Hey, can I ask you something? Did you know anything about serious drugs, the hard stuff? The cops found a needle on Paul yesterday."

"Well, I knew he hated needles and that he tried to, but never could inject himself. I mean, I don't know what else to tell you."

"Do you know anything about some girl at Texaco?"

"No."

"I'm sorry. I shouldn't be asking you all these questions, but we lost touch on the important things. Actually completely lost touch."

"I know. It's okay. I loved him."

"Did he ever get over that man of the house thing with Bob and me?"

"Oh, I don't know. We never talked about it again."

"I never knew that about him until you told me."

"Neither did Jane."

I hug her, taking in the sickening, sweet smell of alcohol residue. The guy with her, the one with the tie, stands back, expressionless. He repositions his hat.

YOUR MOM'S birthday is Tuesday. I know you didn't plan it this way, but she'll never have another good one again, you know that, don't you? Your death, her aging, her mortality, her disappointment and sadness and whatever joy is left in her life will always be linked with this weekend.

Mary from across the street is here. I heard she and Daniel divorced.

"You know," she tells me in the kitchen, "about a month ago, Paul backed into my car, pulling out of his driveway. He knocked on my door and told me about it right after it happened. I was impressed by that. I'm glad he did, too, because I hadn't talked to him in such a long time. And it was the last time. He was a sweet boy. I always liked him." I walk her out and across the street to her house and she gives me a cake. I walk back to the house and stand in a rain that won't let up. It's raining like it knows someone has died. It's an angry rain. I can't go back in the house just yet and have no desire to stand out here, but I am holding a cake in the rain and I am thinking of the song "McArthur Park" which is a song from a million years ago and probably just as well you don't know what I'm talking about. If only I could find a place between the drops. I see cars pulling up to the house. Paul, people liked you, so please tell me this wasn't suicide, please tell me it wasn't because of some notion you had that you were alone or away from love. People can't find parking near the house.

I should stop talking to myself.

I go back inside, back to the wicker chair, and look up at those Playbill posters of Broadway musicals your mom hung over the columns in the living room. I hate musicals. You did, too. Art should depress. How many times will I have to say "Paul died" today? How many times tomorrow and at the service on Monday? How many times for the rest of my life? How many questions will follow about how, when? How much information does anyone want, need? I called Scott to ask whether he's heard from the rabbi, the paper, the morgue in Oklahoma City?

"No, nothing new," he says, "except we're still planning on Monday morning."

"Is Paul coming back today?"

You are not a pronoun.

"Don't know yet."

IF IT ALL works out and the rabbi can get back from Iowa and I can get the paper the information for the service before nine, and your body is returned and your uncle and aunt and grandfather can find flights, the service can be Monday. You hear that? If things work out, my son's memorial service can be Monday and it'll be in the paper. If things are not settled by 9 tonight, Scott will put a notice in the paper that says arrangements are pending. And if the rabbi doesn't make it, and there's a storm in Iowa, and your body isn't returned until Monday, the earliest we could have the service is Tuesday.

Nina just walked in. Drew is standing behind her. She looks determined; he looks lost. He's not going to be able to help her. I meet her in the hallway. She doesn't say anything. I hug her.

"I love you," I tell her. I see your mother.

"What are we going to do about Paulie?" your mother asks in the present tense, hugging her now only child.

Nina doesn't ask what happened. She knows, or doesn't need to know, and they move to the sofa and sit next to each other. Nina then puts her head on your mom's shoulder, but she's not crying. She's not asking questions, not saying anything.

More people. As Nina sits, your mom and I get up to let people in, walk others who are leaving to the door. Food is being brought into the kitchen. Marcia is here, has been it seems since the moment you died, and is taking the food, setting it out, putting the excess in Tupperware. She and your mom are first cousins, but more like sisters. Her sons, too, had trouble with drugs. But they didn't die.

The phone keeps ringing. Your mom is now looking at pictures in an album, telling stories to those around her. I keep waiting for you to waltz in from your bedroom and wonder why all the people are here. Drew is standing by himself. Nina is letting him fend for himself. She is now leaning against the back of Bob's chair. It's leather in a wood frame and it doesn't belong there. Whatever happened to our chair, anyway? I want the chair back. Susan, my wife, called and said she is coming over in an hour or two. She asked whether I think it will be okay if she went to work tonight at another gig she had scheduled.

"Uh, sure."

"Yeah?"

"Yeah."

I don't know what else to say.

What did you think of her, my wife? You once gave me the thumbs up when I asked you about her.

"Better than that other one you were dating," you said. "Susan's gorgeous."

Your approval meant something.

Nina told me she always thought Susan was making too much of the wedding and how you never showed up, always thought Susan held a grudge she didn't deserve to hold.

"Dad, if you forgave Paul, why can't she? It had nothing to do with her."

"Honey, it was insulting to her."

"It was Paul getting back at you—not her."

I forgave you for that, even while it was happening. Still, my best man stood me up. My son stood me up. I remember the rabbi, the same one who will now preside over your funeral, asking me where you were.

"He's not coming."

"That's unfortunate."

Standing there in the rabbi's office the morning of my wedding with my family and Susan's family, I wondered whether they all thought, "How bad of a father is Barry that his own son didn't show up?"

WHILE I WAS STANDING OUTSIDE EARLIER, Vern, Lisa, Mike, Jan, Doug, and Donna, his ex-wife, drove up. When your mom and I were married, we were all close. We had group dinners every few months. We used to argue about many things, but the most heated ones were about *The Big Chill*, which everyone, except me, thought was a beautiful indictment of our generation. I thought it was cheap, lousy filmmaking with a soul-sucking soundtrack. Speaking of films, your mom and I once saw Woody Allen's *Crimes and Misdemeanors*. It's too complicated to explain the plot, but it includes a filmmaker, played by Alan Alda, a pretentious blowhard who hides his superficiality behind a careful guise of wisdom, sensitivity, and erudition. As we were leaving the theatre, your mom was in tears. "That young couple getting married at the end," she said, "has no idea how their lives will change and worsen."

"That's why you're crying?"

"Yeah."

"No," I said, "you cry because that rabbi, that good sweet man is going blind and will never see his grandchildren, and the guy who committed murder gets off and is enjoying his life. THAT'S why you cry."

"What would you know about it?" she asked. "You're the Alan Alda character."

THOSE MEMORIES, too, are in this house today, as are our old friends. They all still love your mom, even if Bob, it seems, has gotten in the way of the actual friendship. Jan, Mike's wife, said she wishes she could have been a part of your life and known you better. More pictures of you are passed around and there are smiles, laughter, shrieks, and some tears, except from Vern and Lisa's boys, Sean and Chris, the twins, who both look pale and sick, sitting off by themselves, near the fireplace. They are a year younger than you. When they were born, I brought their mom, Lisa, a chocolate shake, and we talked about raising boys. When your sister was born, I brought your mom a pizza, which made her vomit.

I bring difficult-to-digest food to women in hospitals when they give birth.

Looking at Sean and Chris, I wonder if it's generational. Is there something in the DNA of twenty-something males that makes you all go through a period of darkness, some misfiring in your synapses that elevates the normal frustrations and difficulties of life into something more desperate, hopeless, and poetically tragic? I want to tell them, "This is not you. This is not going to be you," but of course I don't know, nor, really, do I even know what they're thinking. I asked Mike Selvaggi, the owner of Mario's, one time, after I think the fourth time he fired you—it was eleven times in all—whether he knew what it was.

"When I was Paul's age," he said, "sure, I did drugs, but it wasn't the only thing I cared about. With these kids, that's it. They don't even care that much about fucking. I don't get it."

What did you care about, Paul? What was out there that meant something beyond the normal to you? Were you here, were it someone else's funeral, could you tell me what the looks on the faces of your friends, on the faces of Sean and Chris, mean? How is it some fathers get through to their sons, get their sons through life, and others have to coordinate their funeral service?

BOB and your mom are in the kitchen. I join them.

"Ryan broke down," Bob tells your mother and me, "and said he'd be willing to testify against the girl, the dealer, who injected Paul with the drugs."

"Do we even know that happened?" I ask, instead of begging him to drop it.

"Paul would never have shot himself up," he says.

I hope Bob stops with this.

Someone else, I think a mother of one of your friends, is in the kitchen and hears the conversation.

"This may be a bad time to bring this up," the woman says, "but I read that last night at the University of Tulsa, some eighteen-year-old freshman overdosed on a combination of heroin and oxycodone and that a girl was with him."

"I bet that's the same girl," says Bob.

Oh, for fuck's sake, knock it off.

I don't want to argue with him, certainly not in front of your mother, but it's hard to believe there's this angel of death floating around Tulsa, killing young men. But Bob is convinced.

"I'm going to get to the bottom of this," Bob says.

It's the way he grieves.

After Bob disappears into the office, I hear Donna, Doug's ex-wife, say, "His highs were too high, his lows too low."

Did you do the drugs because you were unhappy or were you unhappy because you were doing drugs? I sound like a character in a bad movie getting drunk on Chardonnay. I wish I could just shut up and be somebody else.

IT'S ABOUT 5:30. I've been here for about 6 hours. Had you known yesterday about the love in this house today, would you have done anything differently yesterday?

A FEW MONTHS AGO, your mother told me that you moved out

of the house. You lived in your car, under a bridge, apparently, and then with Ryan on his dirty sofa at that shitty hotel off the Broken Arrow Expressway. Remember when I went to see you and we went to Church's Fried Chicken?

"Dad, why are we here? I'm not hungry and I don't want to talk."

"I'm your father, that's why we're here."

"Oh, God, not again! What do you want to talk about?"

Weeks later, running a fever, you came back to the house. You stood at the door, shivering, your mom told me, hungry and scared and looking like hell and she let you in. She fed you, put you to bed. She could have, probably should have, slammed the door in your face—after all, you stole from her, lied to her, took advantage of her. But she let you in. How was that not some kind of turning point? When you woke up the next morning, or even as you were falling asleep that night in a warm bed, in your warm bed, did you not think, "This is love. My mom just made me soup and I started the day homeless"?

Where was rock bottom, Paul? If it's not living under a bridge, where is it? If it's not sleeping on shag carpet on Taco's floor at a Value Inn, where is it? If it's not living in an uninsured Jeep Cherokee, where is it? If it's not a courtroom in Baltimore, where is it? If it's not lying on the floor in your room, already groggy and in the early throes of heart arrhythmia with maybe an angel of death standing over you with a syringe, where is it?

If your mom doesn't let you in, maybe you die in the front seat of your car, anyway, amidst papers and bags and drug paraphernalia. She let you in, you overdosed in her house. None of the clichés work. None of the actions, either, that parents are advised to take when their kids are on drugs. You got tough love; you got unconditional love. You were thrown out; you were let back in. You were loved; you were shunned. You had second chances; you were held accountable for your actions. The pablum goes on forever and the problems wouldn't stand still. And now there's Bundt cake and drunk girls in the kitchen and you are ... where are you now? You were loved, though, weren't you? Even you'd admit it. Its power is overrated.

MIKE, our friend from the group, still refers to Ben and James, his sons, as "my boys" and when he says it, he's not self-conscious; he says it with joy. I never referred to you that way. I talked of you, of Paul, but never called you "my boy."

NEAR KRISTIN'S BABY BOY, my two wives are hugging each other again. There are twenty years of my life, two women, two failed relationships in that hug.

They could be friends.

"The baby's beautiful," I hear Susan say, as she and your mom stand over the car seat, cooing over what could be their granddaughter. Nina glares at them both.

Vern, my dear friend, comes over.

"You okay?" he asks.

"Look at that," I say, pointing to the two of them.

"Do I want to know what that's about?" he asks.

"Nah."

Susan and your mom want the baby to be yours. Nina comes over.

"Oh, no," Nina says, sitting in my lap in the wicker chair.

"You thinking what I'm thinking?" I ask.

"Yeah. So, what, they're going to raise what they think is Paul's baby, the two of them, and this is all going to make everything better?"

"I guess. And then they'll fall in love with the baby and then Kristin will hop in a van with some bass player, probably, and move to California, and their hearts will be broken all over again."

"This makes me sick," she says, getting up and heading to the kitchen.

MIKE AND HIS BOYS, Vern and his boys, fathers and sons ... there's a look. In some pictures, some I remember, we have it, too. In one we are standing and your arm is wrapped around my shoulder. We're not looking at each other, but we look like a father and son. Where is that photo? The camera captures the same smile. When you were younger, I felt it, especially when you'd flop into me if we were sitting next to each other, or hear it in your voice when we'd be at dinner and one of your friends would call.

"Can I call you back? I'm with my dad."

My dad.

Last night, between chills and sitting on the toilet feeling my heart rattle, I asked out loud, "How did you let this happen?" I don't know if I was talking to you or myself or God.

Your mom comes into the living room and is now sitting on the sofa. Her arthritis is bothering her.

"Oooh," she winces.

"Can I get you something?" I ask her.

"No."

I ask the others on the sofa, some of whom I don't know, the same thing.

"No, we're fine," one of them says.

I go back to the wicker chair and Susan comes over and crouches by me. "I have to go."

"I understand." I don't.

"It's okay?"

I think she thinks she should stay, but I tell her, again, it's okay. I'm going to meet her later at Ann's, her sister's, after she's done performing. Maybe it's the fear of theft or certainty about humidity, but Susan's guitar goes where she goes, even to the home of her husband's ex-wife when his son dies. It's sitting in the hallway. It makes perfect sense the less you think about it. I walk her and the guitar out to the car.

"My parents are devastated," she tells me.

"And they never met Paul."

How many times to this driveway in the rain today? I'm going to take Nina and Drew out to dinner. We're going to Mario's. How much of our lives revolved around that pizza place? All those Friday nights, when we were all younger, and the three of us would go to Mario's. After you started working there, before coming in, I would just sit in the parking lot and watch you through the front window, marveling at your grin and your mop of blond hair and wait for the sweet, uncertain wave of yours when you would see me come in—the one that would start at your waist and never quite make it to your shoulders. That was our moment. You also pulled a knife on me at Mario's and I heard you tell a friend, describing me, "He's such an asshole."

That was our moment, too.

"Honey, what's the matter?" I ask, as we get in the car. Nina is in the back, next to Drew.

"Nothing, I'm just mad at him."

We would all take you back, Paul, no matter how many needles were found in your pockets, no matter how long we would have to deal with Taco drunk in the front yard and girls with bulimia and babies in car seats on dining room tables.

"He could have stayed here forever," your mom told me yesterday. "I didn't care."

When you'd fall on top of her, flop on her and tell her you loved her, it was worth all the twenties, she told me, that you stole from her, all the lies, the little and big ones, you told her. You manipulated her, but she didn't care. You knew that, too. You ripped her heart out, sometimes for sport, sometimes inadvertently, sometimes because she made it too easy for you not to. But she always forgave you and she never dwelled on any of the moments, any of the grievances. You were still her *Paulie*, still her little boy, still the newborn that took an extra moment to start breathing.

ON THE WAY to Mario's, Nina tells me that she's going back to school after the service, whenever it is. "I love him, I miss him, but I'm not going to stop my whole life." Pulling into the parking lot, I look inside and see Kyle, Mike, and Tim. I see where you should be. We walk in. They all know. I see Mike at the counter.

"I don't know what to say," Mike says. "I don't know."

"I know you don't. Nobody did more for him than you," I tell him.

"No, I didn't. I didn't do enough."

Everyone, Paul, thinks they could have done more for you, better for you. Sitting down, facing Nina and Drew, who are still not saying much to each other, I look at the "art" on the wall, including a framed menu and an atrocious painting of the World Trade Center, to which someone added a draped American flag between the towers after the attacks on September 11. This place, all these years, always so perfectly flawed. The red vinyl seats, often ripped, the formica tables, often chipped, the bathroom, back before the health department made them put in two, in the back, its door opening to a view of the kitchen. On the counter, pictures of Mike, in white, in uniform. There was the pastry counter to the right of the cash register, filled with cannoli and crumb cake, which we loved, and cheesecake, which only Nina did. Mike bought Nina a cake for her birthday one year—went to a bakery in town, and ordered it special. He had cake there but he wanted her to have something special. Next to the pastry counter, the self-serve soda machine. On its face, the index card read *First refill free; Second $.35*. We were special, we never had to pay. I could sit anywhere, that year we stopped talking, and still see you but I liked the tables closest to the register. There I could see you behind the counter, walking in from the kitchen, even if it was just to see your profile near the oven. You were the oven man. There, when I was at those tables, we were less than ten feet apart. I am thinking, too, about the card in your wallet your mom found on New Year's Eve when you turned 14, the one in which you reminded yourself to buy drugs, a scale, a pipe, get in touch with someone. Your mom gave me the card and I walked around my apartment, reading it, trying to make out the penmanship. You needed to remind yourself to buy drugs? Who has to remind themselves that? My son is buying and doing so many drugs, he needs a scale and a reminder. He's 14. How could I be the same dad to you after reading that?

The pizza comes.

"Dad, you okay?" Nina asks.

"Yeah."

WHAT WOULD you have had me do, Paul? What would a good father have done at that point? Forget the card, ignore the vision of you weighing coke in order to sell it? I've only hit two people in my life. When I was in 7th grade, Seth Levy stole my orange juice, so I took my milk and threw it at him. He jumped the table and pounded me in the head with his fist, his ring hitting my eye each time. I hit him back, got in one punch.

The other time I hit someone: you.

When you were 20, and there were new drugs — prescription drugs and those delivered by syringes — I decided not to lose you. I thought I'd stay in your life in case you needed, or wanted, me. You were still doing drugs, I knew that, but I didn't abandon you. You were not going to be able to say, "Fuck you" to me, again — not over that. Through thick or thin and a million other clichés, I was not leaving you this time. You died anyway.

I thought, "At thirty, he'll be better. We'll be better. We'll go to ballgames and take his son, my grandson. Paul will apologize, I'll apologize. It'll be good. He'll be good when he gets to be 30. He'll be good at 30. If only he can get to 30." But maybe that's what a father of a boy he fears will soon be dead tells himself.

It's still raining when Nina, Drew, and I get back to your mom's house. Everyone is gone except Bob and your mom.

"You want to stay with me or your mom?" I ask Nina.

"We'll stay here."

NINA WALKS me out to the car. I make sure she goes inside before I pull out of the driveway.

Every minute of this day has left a mark, but I don't know where the time went. I forgot to call back Scott, the rabbi, or the paper, and nobody called me, so I assume the announcement will say that the service for Paul Friedman, Artist, is *pending*. I am going over to see Susan at her sister's. Ann, whom you've never met you, looks like she's been crying when I get there. She cries easily. I wish I did. Walking into her house, into her kitchen, it feels like my lungs are caving in. I lean against the counter. There's a cancer in my chest.

"I'm so sorry," she says, hugging me.

I move to the refrigerator after the pain subsides. Susan is on her way. Ann doesn't ask a lot of questions, which is good, because I don't have a lot of answers. No, that's not true. I have bad answers. You did drugs, you died.

What answers are there for anyone when a mother of three dies in child birth, when a 12-year-old on a bike is run over by a Ford F-150 going too fast on a neighborhood road, when a 19-year-old girl, putting herself through college by working at a Best Buy, gets raped and murdered in the parking lot? Your death is comparatively easy to describe, to wrap one's head around. You died of too many drugs. You can't blame this one on God, even if one were inclined to do so, which I sometimes am. I mean we set the bar really low for God, if there is one, when it comes to life and death, symbols and renewal. Three thousand people die in a terrorist attack at the World Trade Center and we think there's evidence of an omnipotent God because two of the steel joints used in construction, after falling from a mile in the sky, landed in a form resembling a cross on the street below in front of St. Nicholas Greek Orthodox Church.

Somewhere there's a flower blooming that shouldn't.

Somewhere there's a 6-year-old with bone cancer.

I've been worried about you dying ever since I first heard about you and drugs, ever since I saw that card. I've been worried about getting a phone call from someone, yes, even Bob, telling me you were dead, trying to explain that you're lying somewhere on your stomach next to a laptop. I could hear it, literally, could imagine someone saying, "Paul's dead" whenever I heard the phone ring. When Bob called to tell me, those were his exact words — "Paul's dead" — he sounded just as I thought he would. And I knew it would be a call and knew I wouldn't be the one who found you. I've been rehearsing my drive to your house, as well, and thinking about this weekend and the rabbi and gurneys and people bringing by food and not knowing what to say. My life with you since I saw the note about the scale has been a dress rehearsal for this weekend, and with the exception of dying myself from a heart attack on the toilet or a fast-moving cancer in my soon-to-be ex-sister-in-law's kitchen, it's unfolding as I imagined it would. You died and I was ready for it.

It was your mother who found you.

Details.

Your mom told me that she and Bob were in his office

yesterday afternoon when he said, "Why don't you go check on him? See if he's dead."

He actually said that. And so she went to check.

Someday I'll ask her what if anything went through her mind as she walked past the washer and dryer, through the kitchen, and into the living room, whether she stopped to look at the picture of you on the coffee table or to see what was on television, if she thought she'd find you asleep and if she thought about how she was going to handle you being asleep after promising her you were going to look for a job. How many times had she made that walk to find you passed out, playing video games, sleeping, or not even there?

She told me she saw you face down, tried to wake you, called out for Bob, and then called the police and an ambulance.

"I'm sorry, ma'am, but he's gone," she told me one of the paramedics said when he tried to revive you.

"What? What do you mean?"

"He's gone," the paramedic said again.

How dead were you at this point? Was there a part of you still struggling, trying to tell them to keep pounding your heart, that you weren't dead yet but couldn't talk, couldn't scream out, trapped inside yourself? Could you hear your mother crying? Were you alive when Bob made that joke about you being dead?

Minutes later, Bob called me.

I had just come back from Vegas, was walking in the door and saw his name on my cellphone. I ignored it, put the phone on the kitchen counter, and went to sit with Susan, who was on the sofa. The phone rang again. I ignored it. He called back. "Fuck, what does he want?" I asked her. Again, I ignored it. One more time it rang; once more I sat.

"Aren't you going to see what he wants?"

"It's Bob. I don't want to talk to him."

Another call.

"Okay, let me see."

I walked to the counter, picked up the phone, pressed 1 on voice mail, and leaned against the counter.

"Something terrible has happened." Bob was crying. "Call back immediately. Don't wait."

I knew. Rehearsal was over.

I called back.

"Paul's dead!"

I closed the cellphone and stood in the kitchen. I couldn't take a breath in, I couldn't let one out. I couldn't move. I couldn't stay still. I noticed Susan wasn't on the sofa. She had gone into the other bedroom, but I don't remember seeing or hearing her get there. I walked into the hallway, but stopped midway. There was no power in my legs.

"Honey—" And that's all that came out. I couldn't say your name.

"Honey—" I tried again, but couldn't muster the strength required to say your name. My mouth couldn't form the "P" to your name. It was open but nothing was coming out.

"What is it? What is it?" she said, coming to me. I tried again. I remember her holding me, but I still couldn't say your name. Then, I said it.

"Paul ..."

SUSAN JUST WALKED in to Ann's, leaning her guitar against the front door. That guitar is starting to piss me off, so gentle she is with it, so protective, before coming to hug both of us. We are all in the kitchen, eating licorice and crackers. Ann is cooking something. Life goes on, people get hungry. The rabbi just called. He is back in town. I asked him about a Monday afternoon service and he said that was fine.

"I'd like you, Jane, Bob, Susan, Nina, and me to meet

tomorrow, Sunday, in my office," he said, "to talk about the service and to prepare a eulogy."

A EULOGY—YES, I should give it. Are you okay with that? I know your mother can't, Bob's out of the question, even though he'll want to, and it's not Nina's place. I call your mother, ask her if she can come tomorrow to meet the rabbi. She can. I then call Scott to tell him that Monday is the day and he mentions that you are back in Tulsa, too, having been released by the Medical Examiner's Office in Oklahoma City.

"Really? So everything, everyone is back?" I ask him. "What did they find?"

"The toxicology report won't be back for months."

"Why?"

"They found something, but they won't, or can't, tell me what it was."

"Serious? Drugs, right? There's no surprise."

"Yeah, but I don't know what kind. Yeah, there were drugs."

I call Nina.

"Do you really need me?"

"Yeah, it's important to me, but it's okay if you don't want to."

"I'll think about it."

I call your Aunt Susan.

"Come tomorrow. Tell Wayne and Dad."

"We already were."

It's all working out.

3. SUNDAY

SUSAN and I came home together after Ann's, went to bed together, but slept on opposite sides of the bed, as we usually do. We weren't angry, weren't really much of anything. I'd like to tell you that your death has brought us closer, even temporarily, but it hasn't — unless you want to count the softness I hear in her voice. My marriage is ending and you're dead. I exhale more than I inhale these days. In the morning, we got the house ready, for we're having people over to celebrate/mourn you tonight. Not sure how it was decided or who decided it, but Susan's friends Andrea, Paula, and Stephanie said they'd bring over food and alcohol and make all the other arrangements. They invited, hell, I don't even know, everyone who has any connection to you, me, your mom, Susan, and Nina. With your uncle and aunt and grandfather coming in, we should bring your world, even the parts you don't know or remember, together. It's been fifteen years, I think, since your aunt and uncle and grandfather have seen your mother. I remember your grandmother, my mother, calling your mom after our divorce and saying, "Don't you know the kids are going to resent you for having Bob move in so soon? Wait! Give it some time. What's the rush?" and your mom hanging up on her, as she should have. When I asked your grandmother why she did that, what she thought she would accomplish, she said, "I wanted to tell her what I thought. That's all. I wanted to give her an argument. I'm entitled." When your grandmother died, your mom said that she came to her, called her "Janie," and told her all had been forgiven. You talk to the dead, your mom talks to the dead. I want to talk to the dead.

Two nights, two chances to dream of you, us, and nothing. Why hasn't my subconscious pushed you out, let you in, replayed some moment in our lives? I know what dream I want, too. It would be of us in The Bahamas when you were 11 or 12. You remember? This was the time Nina came with us. We caught the last seaplane of the day from Fort Lauderdale and when we arrived at the hotel, she was so tired, she was literally pounding her hands and feet on the floor. When I told her, "You keep this up, I'm going to send you home," she immediately stopped, looked back at me and said, "Oh, yeah, where you going to get a plane?"

You met girls that week—it was spring break—and got your hair braided by a large Bahamian woman on the beach; snuck into the comedy club and watched your dad tell lesbian jokes and say fuck and make fun of Bob; hung out, probably got high with Mark, whose father, Richard, owned the club; slept one night in the tall lifeguard chair by the Coral Towers with a girl you had just met, something I had done once, too, with a girl from Connecticut; and found the secret code for the VIP room where the food and beverages were free, a room into which I have snuck every year since. I want to see you like that, tanned and smiling with white beads in your hair and coming back to the room just a few minutes after the curfew to which we agreed and to hear you say, "I love you, Dad" before falling asleep. You walked around the island, proud you were there, proud you were the son of the comedian—proud you were my son.

"Hey, Dad," you said, as you walked by me in the Beach Tower lobby one night with some girl you just met and with whom you were holding hands. You waved to me with your other hand, that sweet, self-conscious half-wave, the one I'd see at Mario's.

"That's my dad," I heard you tell her. "He's the comedian at the club."

That was the father I wanted to be, the cool one, the one at whom his son waves and smiles in a hotel lobby in a foreign country and says *Dad* with joy and pride—that father who brings his son to a foreign country and gives him the run of the place. I had a plan. To show you a father who was happy and content with his work and with himself, and I thought if I could do that, if I could be that guy, that dad, you'd see life not as a burden, not even as work, but joy. You'd want to be like me. I thought someday you'd thank me for that and then show your son the same thing.

It wasn't enough.

It was too much.

I wasn't home enough. I missed the every day of the every-day, if that makes any sense, but I gave you The Bahamas. I thought I made up for it. I thought it was better that way. I asked you about it once, whether the time I spent away, working on the road, even if it was a string of one-nighters in Kansas and all you got out of it was a 5-minute phone call from me or a postcard, was okay.

"Dad, all my friends see their dads every day, but it's just at night for dinner or in the morning before school. There's no real time together. At least when you and I get together, we have fun and you take me on trips and we sleep late and eat junk food. I'd much rather have it this way."

You once loved me enough to tell me what I wanted to hear.

• • •

WHAT AM I going to say to the rabbi later today? What I am going to say to your grandfather later? What happens, in fact, when all these worlds collide? I want a sign from you. I want you to shake the walls, whisper my name, something. I want you to enter a dream and stay and I want to sleep a long time. When your grandmother was dying, and I was sitting on the edge of the bed watching her die, as I told you, the hospice nurse took me out of the room and said I should tell your grandmother it was okay to let go, that many people in pain, agony, fight to stay on because they think they're needed.

"You need to tell her it's okay. Tell her you will all be fine, you will all take care of one another," the nurse insisted. "She's in pain. Make it easier on her."

I went back in, up to your grandmother's bed, and whispered, "You can go."

Nothing.

I said it again. Your grandmother, her breathing labored and inconsistent and her mouth slightly open, lay there motionless.

"Mom, it's okay. Let go."

I was about to try again, but your Uncle Wayne, in the room at the time as well, said, "Okay, Barry, enough. Stop saying it now."

He was right.

"Ma, look," I said instead, "if you don't want to go, don't go."

Paul, I mean it. You're gone, but if you're still around, hovering, break a glass, make a window open and close, have a cat jump across the room. Produce a cat. Give me a sign that I can make too much of and endow with too much significance.

I should take a walk, another one, around the university, before meeting the rabbi, but I have too much to do.

I have nothing to do.

The house is already clean, somehow, and the food for tonight is already arriving, so I don't know why I am overwhelmed—of course I do. Meet the rabbi at one; your aunt, uncle, and grandfather arrive around four; people at the house tonight. That's it. I have hours.

YOUR STEPMOM IS GOING to take her dog, Princess Jackie Pie God, the destroyer, and a half dozen other names (don't ask), over to Didi's for the day. I hate the dog. I hate the love Susan gives it, for she has turned into one of those people who endows her pet with every longing, every void they carry around from a life they didn't want but in which they now find themselves.

Susan wanted children. She got a dog.

I shouldn't begrudge her that.

And there's the problem with tense again. Which do I use for you? I have a son, I had a son? I asked Mike yesterday what I should do when someone asks if I have children? Do I answer in the plural?

"You tell them you have a daughter and a son. Two children," he emphasized, "because you do. You always will. Paul's not here, but he's still your son."

ONCE, on stage at the Maxim in Vegas, I asked a woman who was sitting next to a man of approximately the same age how long she had been married. It's a bit I wrote on infidelity and forgiveness and the ledger God keeps when you arrive in heaven.

"Forty-three years," she responded.

"Is that your husband next to you?" I asked.

"Oh, no," she said, laughing, "he's not my husband. My husband died three years ago."

"But you said you've been married forty-three years?"

"That's right."

"When are you going to stop counting?"

. . .

IT GOT A HUGE LAUGH. The comedians in the back of the room were on the floor. She even laughed.

Today, I know why she kept counting.

I'M NOT GOING to walk. The campus of the University of Tulsa is a block away and has, in many ways, been a refuge for me the last few months as my marriage was breaking up. I'd walk through it during odd hours, listening to the saddest music I could find and rehearsing arguments with Susan. I decided to take a drive instead and went to a bookstore near a Chinese restaurant that was near a nursery, which I always thought was odd—the smells of pork and manure and books so closely inter-mingled. The store is named Steve's Sundries, a place that always makes me smile. It has an old-time luncheonette counter in the back. I went for an egg salad sandwich, for God knows what reason, except that an egg salad sandwich at a luncheonette sounded perfect. Steve's is also where I had a book signing when ROAD COMIC came out. Still no reason to be there, except, again, I didn't know what else to do with myself and this place was just the anachronism I needed. As I was walking out of Steve's, my best friend, Dave, out in California, called me back. I had called him on Friday from your mom's. Sitting on the ledge, leaning against the window of Steve's, I told my best friend you died.

"Oh, Jesus. Oh, Jesus. Oh, Jesus," he kept saying. You met him when we were living in a house down by the river at the only time in my marriage to your mother when there was money and happiness. You were probably one, maybe two, and you sat on his lap in that blue chair before we moved it to the house. I always liked that image, even though neither of you looked comfortable. That was an odd house in which we were living when you were born. It had big roaches and was too close to the refinery and the wastewater treatment facility, so when the wind blew to the east, the house reeked of the Arkansas River, hydrocarbons and, literally, Tulsa's shit and piss. One night, you were in your room in your crib and we heard you scream. Your mom and I rushed in and saw you standing, pointing to a large spider or scorpion or something hideous over your bed. I got on a small stool to kill it, but the stool broke and I fell into the side of your crib, making you scream even louder, breaking my wrist in the process. The creature ran away and I was certain you'd never admire me after that.

I'M BACK at the house and Nina just called. She's coming today to meet the rabbi.

"I still don't want to go, but if you want me to, I will."

"I do," I tell her.

"What am I supposed to say?"

"Whatever you want, or don't say anything."

"Fine."

Your stepmom, after I got off the phone with Nina, asked if she should come today, too.

"I really didn't know him that well, but whatever you want me to do. What do you think?"

"Yeah, I want you to come."

"Okay."

EVEN THOUGH THE house is clean, I am now scrubbing the bathtub. There's no reason to think anyone, later in the day, will open up the shower curtain just to see how dirty the tub is, much less care if it was dirty, much less take a bath, but it's something I can do, control, make right. I am using far too much Comet. There are no directions. It says to "sprinkle on wet surface or sponge," but doesn't say how much. It's eleven now, two more hours until we meet the rabbi, and I may asphyxiate myself first. I also just noticed I'm supposed to let the Comet sit on the offending stain for 15 seconds, which I have not been doing.

Susan comes, but drives her own car.

I arrive at Temple Israel first and then, when Susan arrives, we sit on a bench in the lobby outside the gift shop and under an HDTV used to announce bar mitzvahs, weddings, and special events. It's the same bench we sat on when we waited for a meeting with the rabbi before we got married.

"If this doesn't work out," Susan said back then, "let's elope."

Your mom, Bob, and Nina are going to be late.

Susan and I see the rabbi walking out of the kitchen. He, along with temple personnel, are setting up for a cantorial concert, scheduled for later tonight, and I am reminded again about how the world moves on after your death. I apologize for Jane, Bob, and Nina not being here.

"We all need to talk," he says, as he leaves us. "Come by my office when they arrive."

He once told me the best reason to be a good human being was so people wouldn't have to lie about you after you died.

WHEN BOB, your mom, and Nina show up a few minutes later, Susan hugs Nina and then we all walk into the rabbi's office.

"Let's meet in the library," he says, seeing us all at the door. He grabs a yellow ledger pad and we follow him. We take our places around a large table: Nina and your mom on one side; Susan and I on the other; Bob and the rabbi at opposite ends.

We all look at each other.

"So," the rabbi says, "who wants to start?"

Bob says you were a good big brother, a good-looking kid.

"Paul had a tougher time with our divorce than we thought," I say, looking at your mother. "I think that's the first mistake we —no, I—made. I should have understood that. He was only eight, Nina three, so I thought Nina would have it rougher, but I was wrong. That was the first thing I was wrong about."

"I didn't know," your mom says, "that his drug use was that bad."

"I did," I say.

Nina looks disgusted.

"Are you all crazy?" she asks. "He made a hundred and eighty dollars a week; he smoked a pack of cigarettes a day, which is like five bucks. He lived at home, you paid all his bills, Mom fed him, and he was always broke. Where do you think his money went?"

Nina looks at this moment like she wants out of the family. Who can blame her?

Pointing to your mom, Bob, and me, she said, "He told me he knew he had a problem, but you couldn't afford to get him treatment, so don't pretend you didn't know or did everything you could."

Your mom and Bob say, almost in unison, "That's not true."

"Whatever," Nina says, waiving them off, sitting back in her chair.

"Don't do this," the rabbi says, "It's not helpful. Don't do this to yourselves," the rabbi says again, insisting. "It is not helpful. Tell me about Paul," he says to everyone, to no one, hoping to change the subject.

"He had beautiful eyes," I tell him, "before he started using drugs. They were still beautiful, but they changed. They weren't as bright, as clear, as happy."

"He used to help around the house," your mom says. "He was always helpful."

I'm sorry, Paul, we're doing such a lousy job of this. In the time we've been here, all we managed to say about you is that you were an unhappy drug addict with once-beautiful eyes who used to clean up around the house.

Nina looks like she's going to cry. Or stab us all.

And then, as the rabbi is taking notes about how old you were, what high school you attended, Bob says he'd like to say something tomorrow at the service. He wants, he says, to call out the people he thinks were responsible for your death.

"There is no fucking way you're speaking at my son's funeral," I'm about to say to Bob, when someone starts kicking me under the table.

The rabbi is kicking me under the table.

"That's not advisable," the rabbi says, no longer kicking.

Bob seems perplexed, assuming his thoughts would be welcomed. "Why?" he asks.

"Unless," the rabbi says, "you do this, speak in front of people, for a living, it doesn't help," and then he starts kicking me again. "What we try to do," he says, "is give people a sense of calm, to make them feel a little bit better, and it doesn't help if family members are breaking down or calling out others in anger. If you'd like," he says to Bob, "send me your remarks and I will include as much of them as I can. But believe me on this."

And then Nina pulls a piece of paper out of her purse and says to the rabbi, "Okay, I wanted to read this tomorrow, but ..." and then she stops.

"No, go ahead," I tell her. "You can read it. Read it now."

She starts.

"I thought we'd have more time but..." She looks up at the rest of us and continues. "I didn't even say goodbye to you last weekend. I mean, I didn't even go into your room to say good —" And then she starts to cry.

She sits back in her chair. She's done reading.

The rabbi covers her hand.

"See?" he says to Bob, as if on cue. "This is what I'm talking about." He takes Nina's card and puts it inside his yellow ledger pad.

"Can I have this?" he asks.

She nods.

I go around to Nina's side of the table. She leans down, lets me hug her, but it's awkward, uncomfortable. I tell her it's going to be all right.

But it's not.

The rabbi is writing on an angle. He asks if you had been in college, had any hobbies, where you worked.

"What did he like to do?"

I remember the line drawing again and skateboarding.

"Art. He liked to draw."

The rabbi writes it down.

Bob then tells a story about some woman who thought you were sexy and well-dressed when you were twelve, which I don't follow, and how protective you were of your mom and Nina. Your mom isn't talking. Susan is looking down. I tell the rabbi about the time you came over to apologize about not coming to our wedding. I wasn't there, Susan told me about it, and I'm hoping she'll pick up the story, but she doesn't.

"Well, good," the rabbi says. "It's maturity. People grow up."

He wants to know where you worked and what you did. We mention Mario's.

"Where's that?"

"You don't know about Mario's?" I ask. "What kind of Jew are you?"

He smiles. I tell him.

"He was a great oven man," Bob says.

Good God.

It's clear the rabbi doesn't know what that is, but he writes it down and underlines it.

"Paul loved the 23rd Psalm," your mom says.

"That's a good one to like," the rabbi says.

You liked the 23rd Psalm? Since when? And it may be an odd time to remember this, but I remember when I was 13 or so, I got a poster of gargoyles and vines and ominous skies, as well as a woman, and you could see her cleavage and, if I remember right, one exposed breast. I'm not even sure why your grandmother and grandfather let me have it, but I hung it on my wall next to a poster of Bob Gibson, a surly, brilliant pitcher for the St. Louis Cardinals. Anyway, the poster read, and this was in fancy cursive, some sort of gothic font *Yea, though I walk through the valley of the shadow of death, I will fear no evil: For I am the meanest son of a bitch in the valley.* At the time, I thought it was edgy, and a great way to approach life. I'm not so sure it still isn't. A few weeks later in some class, the teacher brought up the 23rd Psalm and read it aloud: "Yea, though I walk through the valley of the shadow of death, I will fear no evil: For thou art with me."

"Excuse me," I said, "that's not it."

"What do you mean?"

"It means you got the ending wrong," I said and mentioned how it should end with the "meanest son of a bitch in the valley."

And now I hear you loved that Psalm. You would have loved that poster.

"We're going to have Paul cremated," your mom continued.

"Are you okay with that?" I interrupt. "Are Jews? I read somewhere that Jews frown upon cremation, either because of The Holocaust, where so many of our people were literally burned to death, or because of some biblical tenet of ours that frowns upon altering the natural decay of the body in death."

The rabbi doesn't say anything, and I'm not sure what we'll do if he refuses do to the service.

"And more importantly," I add, "can we bring the urn into the sanctuary and put it on the bima?"

He hesitates. "That will be fine."

It's important to your mom to have you there.

Just as I'm thinking that, she says, "Well, I'd like it to be there, yes."

JEWS DON'T HAVE open caskets, but now that I think of it, I haven't seen a closed one in the sanctuary, either. Maybe the body is never there. I imagine even this rabbi doesn't know how to turn down a request from a mother who wants her son in an urn at his memorial service. Your mom, too, wants to play your favorite music at the service and is willing to put a collection together, but the rabbi isn't sure the temple has the sound system for it. You loved that Beck song, didn't you, the one with the lyrics, *"I'm a loser baby, so why don't you kill me"*? I'm sure it's never been played at Temple Israel.

Bob again starts talking about what a good guy you are, how much he loved you, tried to help you, but I see the rabbi has stopped writing, so I stand up, thinking we're done, but nobody else does, so I sit back down. When Bob is finished talking, I ask the rabbi if there's any reason officials and attendants from the funeral home need to be there. He says no.

"All right," he says, "anything else?"

I wait for the others this time, and when they do, I, too, get up. I thank the rabbi, who heads back to his office. We all walk out to the lobby. Your mom and Bob are going home. I am going to the airport. Nina wants to come with me, which is what I was hoping she wanted to do. Susan tells me her friends are already at the house, so there's no rush to get back there, but she has some errands to do before people start coming over. I tell your mom and Bob to come by.

"Really?" your mom asks. "We're invited?"

"What, are you kidding?" Susan asks. "Of course. You must come."

This connection between them is sweet and new.

You did that.

Your mom says she needs to go home and lie down for an hour or so, but she'll come over later, she'd love to, but is worried about seeing people. She's the mother of a dead son and the wife of a husband who's an acquired taste. She has a birthday coming up and a son to bury. Her arthritic knees hurt and she wants to make a mixtape. She's stiff, her fingers are curled and swollen, and her movements are slow and labored. When she was younger, she looked like Diane Keaton from Annie Hall. That Jane doesn't exist anymore. It's not just that she got older—we all got older—but there's something transformed about your mother now. I'm not sure I'd recognize her if I didn't know who she was. Watching her walk to the car, I see her grab Bob's arm. I was married to her, she gave birth to you. I watched. I saw you before she did. I heard her say, "Breathe, breathe," when she thought you were taking too long to do so. You were Paul, you were always going to be Paul. And you looked like a Paul. The only Paul there ever was.

I was going to be named Paul. I never told you that.

"DAD, YOU OKAY?" Nina asks on the way to the airport.

"I love you, honey," I say, patting her knee. I'm glad Drew is not with her.

"Love you, too, Daddy."

"What are you thinking about?" I ask.

"I overheard your grandmother yesterday tell someone that Paul was in a better place."

"Really?"

"Yeah."

"I have a feeling it's not going to be the last time we hear it."

YOUR UNCLE, grandfather, and aunt are all coming in on separate flights, twenty minutes apart. Wayne comes first. He's with Hope, his third wife. You'd like her.

"I'm so sorry, Barry," Hope says, as we meet in baggage claim. "I don't know what to say."

I hug Wayne. We don't hug much, your uncle and I. We did the week your grandmother died, but since then, I think something got lost between us.

"I don't know what to say, either," he says, "but tell me what you need. Anything, okay?"

We all go to another gate and see your grandfather who is already walking down the terminal, playing with his cellphone.

"You have to show me how to work this Goddamn thing," he says, as I approach him.

I start to show him, because I don't know what else to do, because I know he'll never stop asking until I do, but he keeps saying, "I know, I know, I know," when I try to show him. His obliviousness is usually filled with a quirky innocence, but today, two days after his grandson died, it's otherworldly. He won't shut up about the phone. We're at baggage claim and he's still playing with it. Maybe this is how he deals with you being dead. Maybe this is how he deals with death.

I'm glad Nina is here, especially glad when I see your Aunt Susan walk from her gate a few minutes later. She hugs Nina, hugs her the way your grandmother would have—big, full, not letting go. Your grandmother was great during tragedies. It was the everyday stuff that leveled her. She used to complain that your grandfather never fought her battles. To her, that was how you loved. "Anyone can love you when things are good," she used to say. Of friends, she always told Wayne, Susan, and me, "You do for your family, not strangers." Aunt Susan grabs my arm at the baggage carousel.

"So ... is dad behaving? He's not, is he?"

I haven't laughed in two days.

"He just asked me to help him with his cellphone."

"Jesus! I miss mom today," she says. "She'd be good. She'd lay him out."

"Yeah, I think so, too, but coming to her grandson's funeral —this would have killed her. She might have been strong this weekend, but she never would have gotten over this. Her first born grandson!"

"She once said, 'I could have more but I couldn't have better.'"

"Mom said that? Our mom?"

"Lying on a raft in our backyard pool, in a one-piece bathing suit, drinking an apricot sour, she said it. I was surprised, too, for this was not a woman who took time in life to smell anything resembling roses."

"But she grew roses."

"That's right, she did. I remember her on her hands and knees in the backyard, planting roses. Damn!"

Your grandfather is trying to access his voicemail when Susan and I get to him at baggage claim.

"Ba," he says, waiting for his bag, "you have to show me how again to set this thing. I read the directions, but I can't figure it out. Okay, just show me. I'll record the message, don't worry about that."

"Dad," Susan says, "not now."

"No, I just want to see how to do it. I can set up the voicemail."

"Dad, drop it!"

"I just need him to show me the voicemail, that's all."

"Dad, stop!" Susan says again, which sounds very much like your grandmother sounded when she'd say, "Jack, stop!"

"All right, all right. I was just wondering how you program this phone and set the voicemail."

She ignores him this time.

They're all staying in a hotel near Oral Roberts University, across from the praying hands and in front of a Wal-Mart, which, as you know, is less than a mile from your mom's, but on the other side of town from my house and Temple Israel. We stop off at my house first before heading to the hotel. They all come in, hug your stepmom who is now back at the house. Susan's friends are here, putting even more food on tables, and the house looks as good as it ever has.

"I'll be back after I take Wayne, Hope, and my sister to the hotel," I tell Susan. "I'll hang around until they're ready and then I'll bring them back. Nina will come with me. I'm going to leave my dad here, okay?"

Your stepmom looks horrified.

"What do you want me to do?" I whisper.

"Don't leave him here," she says. "He's exhausting and I have too much to do."

"Sorry," I whisper back and walk out the door. "Please."

AT THE HOTEL, while Wayne, Hope, and Susan go up to their rooms, Nina and I sit in the hotel lobby and watch people in the bar, laughing and drinking. I look at myself in a mirror in the lobby, wondering if I look like a man who has just lost his son, wondering what a man who just lost his son looks like. Is there a scar that develops, a strand of gray hair that develops overnight, a tremor? What mark is left on a person without a child? I don't drink, you know that, but I wish I did. I wish I had a vice this weekend.

RETURNING TO THE HOUSE, driving down Florence Avenue, I see cars that I recognize: Didi's; Paula's, Rick's wife, from the restaurant; Ed and Anita, my uncle and aunt, your great-uncle and aunt. It looks like they've all come for a party. There's comfort in recognizing cars that I know.

Tonight, I want noise and music and a house full of shrimp

and cheese and beer and people who spill stuff in the living room and who won't know whether to cry or laugh. I want to run out of chairs and not think about what kind of father I was. I want anyone who mattered to you, me, your mom, Nina to be there. It's human contact I'm after. As I walk into the house, I notice you are everywhere but nowhere. The people here, these friends of your stepmom's, those dusting furniture and arranging deviled eggs and putting cakes on platters are there because of you. Even if they only know me, or your mom or stepmom, there's no distinction anymore between any of us. Your grandfather, sitting in the living room, has a plate of food. It's filled high. He doesn't get up when I walk in. Your step-mother looks exhausted.

"Your dad just drains me," she says, as she pulls me aside, as if I didn't hear her before.

We walk to the kitchen.

"I see where you get it," but she's not smiling when she says it.

Looking at your grandfather, I wonder when, if, he'll come and talk to me. He's sitting there, close to the food, and I hear him talk to others as they walk by him. I'm a father today. I'm a son today. I'm here, he's here, but he's now on his second plate of food and he needs his voicemail set up. I see him pick a deviled egg off his plate. He gets up, gets another, sits back down, crosses his legs, eats it with fervor. I wonder what he needs, what he's thinking, whether he sees the moment: the grandfather, the father, the son.

"Dad," I call, "you need anything?"

"Something to drink, a Pepsi. Thanks."

He answers me. It's not any more than that. He's thirsty. The missing part of the chain now, the grandfather, father, son —no, that's not the problem. He's thirsty and wants a Pepsi.

I bring my father a Pepsi. "Here you go."

"Thanks," he says. "So much food," he says. "How many people you got coming?"

"I don't know."

"But how many do you think?"

"I don't know"

"A lot?"

"I don't know."

"You got enough chairs?"

"Yeah, I think."

"You know all these people?"

"Yeah."

How can you be angry? He's 82. He's here.

You know about fathers missing moments, don't you?

WHEN YOU WERE at culinary school in Okmulgee, Oklahoma, after we made up, I used to come with snacks and cash. I bought you a microwave. It was one of those second chances you weren't supposed to have, getting in that school. You didn't finish high school, but then you got a GED. Somehow, this culinary school, one of the best in the region, with open admission, is available. You get in, get financial aid, your mother and I make up the difference. If you had stayed for two years, you would have received automatic acceptance to the University of Oklahoma or Oklahoma State. If all that had happened, you could have graduated from college. You'd be just like everyone else then, everyone who studied and graduated. All you have to do is go to class—cook, in this case—do what they tell you. You don't. After one semester, you leave. Forget the money, forget the culinary career. Those things weren't important. It was you and staying with a thing.

One semester.

You come home and you move back in to your mom's house. You got your job back at Mario's. You and I are okay. Not the same, not good, but better. One day, your mom and you were going to lunch to talk about your future and you asked me to come.

Chili's.

"What are you going to do now?" I asked. "Why do you keep doing this to yourself? I mean, you can't keep blaming us for things."

"I don't," you said.

"Don't you, though?"

I don't know why I said that. You really hadn't, Nina even told me, "Paul doesn't blame you, Dad."

"Okay, Dad, you want to know why I hated you, why I did the things I did to you?"

"No, I don't."

That's all I ever wanted to know. That's all I want to know now. That's what this elegy is about. That's what my whole life with you was about. But I had to make a point. I had to be a prick, one of those fathers who takes no shit from his kids. That's the role I insisted on playing at that moment, the father I decided I had to be. I wanted an apology, an acknowledgment from you about all the work I did, all the indignities I suffered. It was cinematic, Paul, a pose. That's what the script in my head called for.

I'm sorry.

You were deflated. I saw you sink within yourself. How much that must have taken out of you just to ask me that, to bring this up in front of your mother, to talk about fathers and sons and the distance between them, between us. And what did I do? Swatted you away. I was going to show you that your self-discovery meant nothing. Get a job, career, life, then come talk to me. A good, strong father will not allow his son to wallow in self-pity, because a good, strong father, the father I wanted to be, says that. That one moment that could have changed our lives, your life, maybe have even saved it and all I had to do was be your father and say yes.

"Forget it," you said. "Fucking unbelievable."

IT'S TOO LATE, you're dead, cremated, in an urn, but what were you going to say, what were you going to tell me? Were you going to tell me about what it was like to be eight years old and not be the man of the house? Were you going to tell me about the time I talked you out of playing football? Were you going to tell me the time the 4th grade teacher picked you to tell the other kids about growing up in a divorced household and you said to them, "Deal with it, that's all"? Were you going to scream at me for deciding to stop talking to you over the drugs and how much that hurt, how it stung when I came into Mario's with Nina and ate and laughed and never said a word to you? Were you going to tell me about losing me, your best friend, and how life, which was never good to begin with, got worse?

That's why a son tells his dad to fuck off, isn't it? Because the father deserves it, because the father won't hear the explanation from the son, won't listen to him at all, even when he gets another chance in a booth at a restaurant. When I hear people, good people, many in this house right now who will tell me that I wasn't a bad father, I want to believe them—and sometimes I will— but then I think back to that afternoon. How many chances does a father get to get it right with his son?

YOUR GRANDFATHER IS STILL EATING. The food keeps stacking up. People pass me, stop, touch my arm, hug me.

Andrea and Stephanie, the friends of your stepmother, are in the kitchen. They make me smile, both of them, as Andy Martin is married to a guy named Dean; Stephanie Stewart is married to a guy named Jimmy. I know those names don't mean anything to you, but trust me when I tell you that knowing Dean Martin and Jimmy Stewart is pretty cool. The house is alive, Paul, with people in every room, standing against walls, sitting on floors. Some are on the front porch; some, like your sister, out back. The house is bursting wide open. Your grandfather hasn't moved. I am in the kitchen, standing next to a plate of asparagus, I think, and your Aunt Susan keeps rubbing my back, as your grandmother would have.

"Oh, Barry," she keeps saying. "You going to be okay?"

YOUR MOM JUST CALLED, apologized for being late, and wondered how long it would be going on.

"I hope all night."

"Is it okay if we still come?"

"Yes."

I need air.

Nina is standing out back, near one of the beer coolers, smoking, and drinking a Corona. She is clearly drunk.

"Hey, sweetie."

"Hi, Dad."

"Is Drew coming?"

"I don't want to talk about it."

"You sure?"

"I just called him. I woke him up."

"Not good."

"No, it's not. Fuck him!"

She just opened another beer. I think I'll come back later.

Your grandfather is talking to Andy, who's laughing. I see him offer her something off his plate.

"Your dad's a riot," Andy tells me when I meet her in the kitchen. "I see where you get it."

Your stepmom's parents wanted to be here, but Dayne, her dad, has emphysema and has trouble walking, though he told

Susan he is coming to the service tomorrow. This from a man who needs to sit down on trips between the bedroom and living room to catch his breath. You're dead, he's dying. You never met them, though Ellie, that's Susan's mom, said she wished she had met you. "I could have straightened him out," she said. She and Dayne, most days, sit and watch Fox News all day just to annoy me. There was so much about my life, after your mom and I divorced, as there was about yours, that was a mystery. I would have invited you to dinner over there, as I did Nina, and you would have been bored, as she was, but that's what fathers do to their sons. You would have had these moments to remember with your son, my grandson, perhaps while tucking him in some night, where you told him stories about how I bored you. You would have thought, while seeing your son fall asleep and maybe while you were stroking his hair, "My dad used to do this with me, tell me his stories." You might have even told him one of my stories, and then, later, after he was sound asleep, your son, your daughter, you would have called me and told me about it. And then your wife, or mine, would see us on the phone and smile that we still talked, that there was still a connection, that a grandson was asleep and that a son called his father to tell him. And that would have been the moment that the link between us, you and me, between your grandfather and me would have been set, locked, resolved. We would have continued the chain between fathers and sons, a chain that didn't start with us, that didn't end with us.

Except it did.

You didn't want kids, anyway, right? Nina doesn't, either. You don't mind if I take that personally, do you?

Still more people are coming in now with more food. The kitchen counter is full. There's something with marshmallows, something else with beans, a taco dish, macaroni and cheese, a roast, a ham, chicken, too many desserts and bottles of soda and wine, some beer. It all smells so good, but I can hardly taste any of it. It smells like a party, your grandfather is right. Mike and Jan just arrived. Vern, Lisa, and their twins are here, too. Sean and Chris still look troubled. Why is this bothering them so much? Your mom called again and said she will be even later. Would it still be going on when she gets here?

"Yes, it will. Even if it's not, come," I tell her.

She, again, thanks me for inviting her.

"Nina still outside?" your Aunt Susan asks.

"Yeah."

"Go out there, Barry."

I do as I'm told.

She's drunk, your sister, very drunk.

"Honey, did you talk to Drew again?"

"He's tired. He's not coming." She takes a long drag of her cigarette, exhales in my direction while shaking her head. Your sister just blew smoke in my face.

"Look, sweetie, cut him some slack. His brother died a year ago and maybe he just can't do this again. I'm sure he loves you. Don't be so hard on him. My father, your grandfather, doesn't know what to do, either, what to say."

"Oh, fuck that, man! If my leg was amputated, I'd be there for him. Fuck that! I was there every moment for him and he can't be here tonight? Tonight? Fuck. That."

I go back in the house now and see your aunt.

"How was she?"

"Fine, fine! Go see her."

More people still. Still more food. A turkey, a big one, covered in tin foil.

Your mom just walked in. She's smiling. Your grandfather gets up and joins your aunt and uncle in greeting her. Everyone hugs. Bob is with her, as is her mother, your grandmother. Your mom finds a seat in the living room and someone brings her a plate of food. The last time she was here, she and Nina were arguing, as Susan was trying to give a guitar lesson. Your mom chased after Nina, through the house, screaming at her. Later that night, Susan mentioned how it was all too much sometimes. You have brought all these people together, Paul, and you are everywhere—in conversation, in memory, in silence, in the laughter, in the places you've never been. I move from room to room looking for ... what? It's motion, that's all it is. I have nowhere to go, but I keep heading in that direction and am in a rush to get there. I want to be seen. I want to disappear. There are so many people here, my home doesn't look familiar but it's warmer than ever. Those who can, look at me; those who can't, stare down at their plastic plates. Some move away, some come closer. Smiles, tears, vacant stares. Some, when they see me, let me know why they're here; some mouth your name. Some mouth mine.

You're alive and I died.

Uncle Ed just came into the kitchen and asked, "How you doing?" And just as he did, something happens. I hug him and I won't let go. I don't know what I was trying to say, but I can't stop shaking. I am trembling and can't stop. I am breaking apart from the inside. I don't know how I'm breathing because I can't feel air. Ed and I are standing not far from where you sat the last time I saw you, when I made you a hamburger. I liked watching you eat hamburgers, liked seeing you devour them in two or three bites and then sit there, wherever we were, and stare at me and mine until I gave you half. Remember the recipe we used from *The Godfather*, the one Clemenza tells Michael about? How the secret was to add red wine and a little sugar to the meat? Those burgers I made were our last meal together. It was about a month ago. You came over, sat at the kitchen counter, and showed me your new computer, while I brought out the George Foreman grill, a grill everyone hated except you, me, and Nina. There's an unopened 32-ounce bottle of Del Monte Ketchup in the refrigerator. Someone must have brought it over, since we don't use Del Monte. You, Nina, and I refused to use Del Monte. It had to be Heinz. I know it wasn't there before, because I never have two bottles of ketchup in the house. That was our deal, remember? The passage of time must be measured in ketchup bottles. The big bottle of Heinz, the one you and I bought a year ago, is still half full. When I came back from California, a year after the divorce, we went shopping for the first time and bought our first bottle. It lasted three years. We used to make a big deal every time we needed a new one. We only made it through four and a half bottles before you died. What's that: fourteen years, a little over four bottles? Even through the years we weren't talking, I never bought one without you. Somehow our reconciliation and my need for ketchup coincided, which I find at the moment, reassuring. But now with this new bottle, this impostor inside, this Del Monte, it's just a condiment now. Your life in ketchup bottles, and there's no reason to count anymore.

You asked if I had a copy of *Microsoft Word* that last meal you had here. If I did, could you borrow it, could you take it with you when you finished your hamburger? There was no reason for me to have a copy, certainly no reason to have one at the kitchen counter behind some mail, but I did. A friend had coincidentally and inexplicably dropped off a *Word* disc the previous day and asked if I wanted one.

"Sure, I'll never use it, but put it there," I indicated by the mail.

"Paul, move that letter by the phone."

"Dad ... Wow! You have one! And you have one here."

"Yeah, how about that?"

"It's right here!"

"Take it. It's yours. Who's the best dad in the world?"

"You are."

I watched you eating. I wanted to come over to your side of the kitchen counter and hug you and assure you that nothing would ever again happen to Paul Friedman, my son, from now on, for your father would always have what you needed close by.

Sorry.

Ed keeps hugging me. We should have had moments like this, you and I, where all the nastiness, all the misunderstanding, could have been smothered, where there was nothing but the future and the best of the present. We could have just stood there, Paul. I wouldn't have let go this time. I made you another hamburger. You devoured that one, too.

I have been holding on so tight I think I'm hurting Ed.

"Thanks. I'm sorry," I say, kissing his neck. "I'll let you go."

"You going to be okay? I can stay."

"No, thanks. I'm fine."

I DON'T KNOW what a seizure feels like, but mine's over, and I can feel my lungs contract and expand.

I see your mom, sitting at the dining room table, smiling. She is smoking. Wayne, Hope, Susan, and your grandfather are all standing around her. Your mother has a laugh, almost a cackle, when she's happy and I've heard it a few times tonight. I almost forgot how much she loves company. She looks like she's been starved of it. I can see Bob talking to Stephanie and Andy and they're smiling. I hear your grandfather say to nobody in particular, "You know, everyone here, together, it's nice. It's a shame we have to get together at times like this though."

MIKE AND JAN come into the kitchen and ask if I would come outside with them to see Mike's parents, who want to say hello, pay their respects. I don't know if you remember Francis and Jack, Mike's parents, but we used to go over to their house in Verdigris, Oklahoma, for Independence Day and set off fireworks in their backyard by their chicken coop and pool. The parents would sit on folding chairs and direct the proceedings, while you and Mike's kids and what seemed like hundreds of others lit cherry bombs and rockets and then ran away when the explosives started. The Honakers always asked about you, even when I didn't have anything to tell them.

I walk to the bottom of the driveway to where the car they're in is idling. Francis is the first one out. She's behind the driver. She's on crutches, so she leans against the door as I hug her.

"I'm sorry, doll. You know we love you. And we love Paul."

Your grandmother called me *doll*, too.

"Yeah, I know. Thank you for coming."

I see Jack getting out the front passenger side and he, too, is in visible discomfort. He's a big man with a bad heart. He was a doctor when he was younger, a country doctor. I go around to meet him.

"Sorry, Barry, it's terrible," he says, leaning on my shoulder. "We just wanted to come by, let you know—"

"I know. And I don't know how to—"

"We'll be there tomorrow," he says. "Now go back inside."

They struggle to get back in the car, first Francis, then Jack, both in so much pain that Mike and Jan have to help them into their seats and buckle them in.

IN THE HOUSE, Bob is helping your grandfather program the cell phone. Nina, who's now inside at the dining room as well, is laughing with your mom, who is also now clearly drunk. It's not a bad sight, mother and daughter drunk. It's just one I never thought I'd see in my living room at a party in your dead honor.

"Am I seeing what I'm seeing?" Aunt Susan says, pointing to Bob helping your grandfather with the phone.

"I think so."

"I'm going to kill them both."

Some woman I don't know just came up to Nina and said something that made your sister wince.

After she leaves, your aunt and I go over.

"What did she say, honey?" I ask.

"Oh, what do you think? She just said that Paul was in a better place."

There it is.

"How did you respond?" Aunt Susan asks.

"I didn't. I just looked at her."

"Nina, honey," she tells her, "if anyone says that to you again this weekend, you have my permission to smash their head against whatever wall you're closest to. Just tell them your aunt said it was okay."

That makes both of us laugh.

YOU CAN'T BE in a better place, for there is none better. I don't know what in heaven, literally or figuratively, could be better than people you love and people who love the people who love you in a house with this much love and food and laughter—this house. Watching these people, Paul, seeing what they've done for your mom and me, how they stopped their lives for us, it's impossible to think there's some place where there's more love, more compassion, more selflessness. This is the better place, if anyone would stop to think about it, that can't be improved. It is a place you would love to spend your life. I see white wine glasses on the fireplace, half-eaten plates of cheese and cakes and garnishes on the floor, people sitting on the arms of sofas and chairs, Sean and Chris by themselves, your grandfather and stepfather playing with a cell phone. But I see something else, too: your stepmom, my wife, in a bandana, boots, and a long brown burkha that runs the length of her body, walking through the living room, hugging and kissing people and thanking them, on her way out the door, a guitar strapped to her back.

4. MONDAY

I HAVE THE BLACK SUIT, dark gray shirt, and black tie laid out on the bed. In the movie *Ordinary People*, the wife sees what her husband is wearing to their son's funeral and tells him to wear a different shirt. He changes but years later remembers the moment and is furious. Why would she care about such a thing? Who would even notice?

Your son dies and you have to iron.

What do you think? Should I wear the suit—the suit, by the way, that I wore when Susan and I got married—the one you never saw?

The one you still won't see.

THE MEMORIES, Paul, come in perfect shards, like the broken glass that comes from a smashed windshield, the kind mandated by law not to shatter. I can see them all, the vast majority, anyway, in a shiny pile in front of me. Touch one, a small cut; touch another, a hemorrhage; touch a third, scarred for life.

AFTER HER GIG LAST NIGHT, after the party was over, Susan

went to Didi's, picked up the dog, and went upstairs to sleep. It's where she is now. I'm standing in baby blue boxer shorts, looking at the clothes I'm going to wear to my son's funeral.

I don't have to get dressed now. Your service isn't for hours, but I once again don't know what to do with myself. I can't keep walking around this house in my underwear. Or maybe I will. It's my house, my underwear, my son. I am now looking at myself in the closet mirror that your stepmom cracked once throwing her hair straightener across the room when she discovered we were not having children.

I never repaired the mirror.

"I have some rage," she said at the time.

I WISH I could remember how to make a Full Windsor. Like diving into a pool and riding a bike, it's a skill you're not supposed to forget how to do, but somehow I have. Who forgets such things? I used to know how to do both. A half Windsor it will be. It looks fine, albeit uneven. But how good does a father have to look on a day like this? I'm dressed, the shirt is fine, the tie is fine. I didn't iron.

I checked the bathtub. I did a good job yesterday.

MY WEDDING DAY, once more, and I'll drop it. We were over everything by then. You said you were coming, you said you'd be my best man. I sat on the sofa at the house, waiting for you to come by. We were going together, remember? That was important. I called your mom.

"Do you know where Paul is?"

"No." She was lying. You were in the same room with her, I found out later.

All you had to do was stand there with me.

. . .

I DON'T WANT to read. I don't want to eat. I don't want to sit. I don't want to stand. I am now in my suit and still walking around the house. I open and close the refrigerator door, look at myself in the bedroom and bathroom mirror to see, again, if there's any lasting imprint on my face now that you're dead. I walk back into the living room, see Jackie, Susan's rat terrier with the impossibly long name, sitting on the chaise. I pet her. I never pet her. She looks confused. I don't blame her. A dead son, a dead Paul, these wedding day clothes, a little dog who doesn't know why she's being petted by a man who never pets her. I heard your mother yesterday say she was "burying my son" on Monday and it made me think, once again, of those shovels and caskets and straps being lowered into the ground. At your great-grandmother's funeral, the straps around her casket couldn't be extracted after they were lowered into the ground. The gravediggers pulled, jerked. Nothing. The funeral director, detecting that the moment was getting away from the dead woman in the casket and from the people there to honor her, nodded, and the two gravediggers jumped into the hole and retrieved the offending tethers.

I'LL HAVE a stroke if I stay here. I keep finding mirrors. I don't remember having that many. There's a mirror in the dining room. I am trying to avoid my wife, trying to find her.

I'M GOING to the Temple.

"Honey, the service isn't until one. Don't go now," Susan says when I tell her I'm leaving.

"I can't sit," and then I lie. "Scott, the guy from the funeral home, said he was coming early and I want to make sure I'm there to meet him."

"You want me to come with you?"

"No, thanks. I think I want to be alone."

That's not true. I want her there.

THE TEMPLE now has leather chairs in the lobby in a V.

"Yeah," the rabbi told me once. "Victory! Just like the charismatic Christians have. What's the matter with you?"

I sit in a wing of Victory. The Temple building is not empty. There are people cleaning up from that concert I told you about. They are removing flowers, centerpieces, but nobody, as yet, is here for you.

I SEE the rabbi coming out of the kitchen.

"What are you doing here so early?" he asks.

"I didn't want to be late."

He smiles. "You okay?"

"I didn't have anywhere else to go."

"This is a good place to be then."

And then, Paul, the rabbi did something he's never done in the thirty years I've known him: he extends his arms. He hugs me.

"Sorry," I say, even though I don't know if he knows I'm crying, as I back away.

"It's okay, okay. Listen, about what Nina wrote," he says, "I can't—" and he starts to choke up. "I ... can't say it. It's between a sister and a brother. It's beautiful, but it's not for me. I'm going to give it back to you, but please let Nina know I think it's beautiful."

"We are thinking," I tell him, "of going to The Bahamas and sprinkling Paul's ashes in the ocean in a few months. He liked it down there. We all remember him being happy. Maybe she can say it then."

"That would be perfect," he says. "I have some things to do, but you sit here as long as you like." I watch him walk with that slight limp of his down the corridor to his office, past the boards of dead Jewish names, some illuminated by lights. When it's their Yahrzeit, the anniversary of someone's death, the little Christmas-like bulbs (which is a terrible way to describe them) that bracket their names on the plaque are turned on. Six or seven other names are illuminated; six or seven Jews in Tulsa with whom you'll share a Yahrzeit. During the time of these anniversaries, the names of the deceased are read by the rabbi in the sanctuary. Maybe it's the acoustics in the room, but the names hang in the air and evaporate just as he reads the next name. The two names barely occupy the same time and space. It's a fist tap, of sorts, a kiss on the cheek. One ascends, one descends. The whole process takes about a second and a half.

HERE'S the rest of what your sister wrote:

I wish I could say I lost my best friend on Friday afternoon. Paul had finally seemed like he was doing what he always wanted. Paul was in Maryland, he loved the East Coast. He wanted me to visit, but I started college in August and I just didn't have time. Being 5 1/2 years apart — me and Paul were never close, but we were finally getting to the age where we could relate. I guess I figured we'd have time to be friends when I was done with school. I know Paul knows I love him. I just wish we had more time.

Notice the present tense. "I know Paul knows I love him."

I look up and see the rabbi standing there again. "I see what you mean," I say, indicating the letter. "By the way, I'm sorry about that thing with Bob yesterday and wanting to speak."

"No, he actually faxed me something. It was pretty good, too long, but some of what he said needs to be said, but just not here, not today."

The rabbi goes back into the temple kitchen. I get up, walk around the lobby, looking at the books outside the gift store and the Bar Mitzvah announcement on the message board. I walk into the sanctuary and see an empty room, a red wall behind the ark, and light coming in through stained glass. I go into the back of the kitchen where you and I used to sneak after Friday night services to buy Cokes from a machine that few people knew was there. While everyone else was forced to drink iced tea and lemonade with their challah bread and crumb cake, we had cans of Coke.

The machine is gone.

I walk outside and around the building, into the playground where your mother and I first dropped you off when you were two and we enrolled you in pre-school. Miss Tucky ... Miss Ann. I remember your teachers' names. You loved them. For the first time in three days, there's no rain. People are starting to arrive, some from the Temple, your extended Temple family, as the rabbi likes to call them, who were notified in an email. The announcement in Sunday's paper about the service did say *Pending*. Today's paper gave the details of your life. It did not say you were an artist, though. A woman whose name I can't remember just came by to say how sorry she was.

"You don't remember me, I know."

"No, no, I do," I said. I don't.

She smiles.

"You don't, Barry. It's okay. I'm so sorry for your loss."

She leaves without telling me her name.

I SEE VERN, Lisa, Mike, and Jan pulling up. Some people from TulsaPeople, the magazine where my column appears, are here, as well. This morning, I wrote to Michelle, a photographer and my friend, to tell her. She wrote back and said, "I hate that this has happened to you," which I thought was sweetly perfect. Missy and Kendall, two of the editors, and Ace, another photographer, have come, too, but Michelle is different. I have a crush on her. As she hugs me, I realize it's the first time I've ever actually touched her. I find myself smiling. I have you to thank for that. Bob, Nina, and your mom walk in and your mom sets up a placard in the lobby of pictures of you: some with Nina, some by yourself, some with her and Bob. There are none of you and me. How can that be? In one, you must have been three or four, in pre-school, here at Temple Israel, and you're in some costume wearing a hat and vest and sash and you're with your classmates—it's something called the Sunshine Generation—and there's a corsage on your lapel. You're looking away from the camera, but your arm is around a girl sitting next to you and you have this smile, so broad, so sweet, a smile you never should have lost, a smile that should have inoculated you from a day like this.

That's my son with a cardboard yellow sun on his lapel.

Bob, wearing a leather jacket, has just placed a D.A.R.E canister on a table outside the sanctuary, near the placard your mom put up. Scott from Fitzgerald's is here now, too. He has you in a felt container inside a plastic black box.

"Is that Paul?" I ask.

"Yes."

I follow him into the sanctuary and watch him place you on a small table at the bottom of the steps that leads to the bima. There is one photo of you, the main one people will see, for it's center stage. You must be around nineteen or twenty. It's blurry, both you and the picture, and I can see the decay all around you. Your left eye is drooping; your right one is looking past the camera. You're sneering. Your complexion is hard and looks like it has catalogued every drug you ever took. This photo and the ones of you as a member of the Sunshine Generation cannot be the same person. I move you, the box of ashes, to behind the photo and lean the photo against it. I want people to see you alive, even in this picture, not dead, in these ashes. There are flowers here, too, three arrangements, on another small table, but there's no note on any of them. I ask Scott if he's going to stay and he says he is. We're going to enter the sanctuary from the auditorium. Your friend Adam just handed me your red Phillies' hat, the one I got you at Veterans Stadium.

"Where did you get this?" your mother, who has come up to greet him, asks.

"I just had it," he said. "I don't know."

I bought it for you. You, your grandfather, and I went to Veterans Stadium and it was raining. We were getting drenched, eating peanuts and nachos and drinking large Sprites and watching baton twirlers and local bands out on the field kill time during the rain-delay and you needed a hat. When the game re-started, The Marlins scored eight runs in the first two innings and the fans started booing. It was funny, wonderful, especially when the fat guy behind us screamed, "Come on, Phils, this ain't the fucking Yankees, it's the Marlins for Chrissakes! Play ball, would ya?"

You kept the hat all this time?

It's dirty, sweat-stained, and has lost its shape, but it's here.

What about that jacket, the gray Diesel brand, you wore all the time? I want it. I will wear it if I can find it, even if Jews believe it's bad luck to wear the clothes of the dead, even if I don't look good in it. We're about the same size now.

THE SERVICE IS about to start. Scott and the rabbi show us how we'll proceed into the sanctuary. It's the same path your stepmom and I entered when we got married. There are too many people back here, not just family, about to walk in together. What difference does it make? Wayne, Hope, your grandfather, and your aunt just arrived. Ed and Anita had lent them one of their cars, so they drove themselves from the hotel.

Your Aunt Susan looks like she's ready to punch someone.

"What happened?" I whisper, as she walks up to me.

"Later," she whispers back.

WE'RE ALL HERE NOW. The rabbi takes his position and we all follow him inside. As we enter the sanctuary, people stand. I try to smile and thank everyone I pass, try to make eye contact. I see that Jack and Francis Honaker, Mike's parents, are here, as they said they would be, standing, both supporting themselves by holding on to the pew in front of them. Jack smiles at me and then wipes off his glasses. He's in pain just standing there. This is our time, Paul, yours and mine. I am sitting on the seat closest to the center aisle. You stepmother is next to me, your mother next to her.

The sanctuary is full, which surprises me. Your friends are sitting in the back, towards the door. They have all walked in with the same lumbering, lazy glide they walked into your house the last few days, the same gait they all seem to have worked so hard to perfect. They are not dressed up; they're not dressed down. Your death didn't affect their fashion. Nobody looks like he or she has changed for your memorial service. I guess that's the way you'd want it, but as I see one of your friends in a black fedora and black jeans with a long chain and a Nine Inch Nails T-shirt, I wonder what moment in your life, if any, makes you change your clothes ... makes you want to. They're emotionless, too, sitting there, all of them. Why don't you mean more to them? Why are none of them crying?

Like your grandfather, though, they're here—that's important.

The rabbi and cantor are in position on the bima. You, your ashes, your picture, between them. A piano starts playing something funereal. Your mother made a mixtape and brought it, but as the rabbi told her, it couldn't be played. After some Hebrew, some responsive reading, the rabbi pulls out a manila folder and opens it. I put down the prayer book. I want to hold your sister's hand but I'm too far away. I strain to see her, but she's not looking in my direction. The rabbi begins, prefaces his remarks, by talking about God's mysterious ways and making moments count and touching loved ones.

I'm already not impressed.

And then:

"God of all life, our hearts are grieved beyond the power of expression. In the face of this kind of tragedy there are no words to mitigate the pain or to console the inconsolable. We have come to mourn for the years Paul did not live."

No, that's not it, not entirely, I think to myself. We've come to mourn for the years you did, too, the sad ones, the bad ones, which, as it turns out, were most of them. The rabbi is straining to find your life.

"Paul's 24 years were surely too few, but they surely were not empty. As those who most shared Paul's life rolled back the years with me yesterday, good memories emerged — sixth and seventh grade football teams, skateboarding, cooking, video games, and art. Paul had pages and pages of an unfinished line drawing on graph paper through which he expressed what he could not express otherwise about his life. Yes, there were struggles with school and with relationships, times when Paul seemed bewildered by the world. But there were also years of successful work as an oven man at Mario's."

For Chrissakes, successful work as an oven man?

"Paul believed in God and prayed. You told me that the 23rd Psalm was one of his favorites. This poem is known by heart by millions of people—Christians and Jews alike. It is recited by innumerable individuals when they find themselves in a situation of pain or trauma. Let me share with you again just a few lines of this Psalm. 'The Lord is my shepherd, I shall not want ... Though I walk through the valley of the shadow of death I shall fear no evil, for Thou art with me.' Friends, I believe this Psalm has captured the emotions of so many people because it helps us traverse the highway of pain and trauma, agony and suffering, and return to the roadway of normal life. There is a central lesson to be learned from this Psalm. 'Though I walk through the valley of death, I will not fear.'"

And because I am the meanest son of a bitch in the valley.

I feel myself smiling. This wasn't your favorite passage; it's your mom's. Her projection, her wanting it to be yours is what your mother wants right now. You believed in God? The Vikings believed in God. Odin was their God. I think you know all this.

The rabbi continues:

"People who don't have trouble getting through life will never fully understand those who do."

That's it! That's what I have come to hear.

There's then a story about thorn bushes and beautiful roses and how some see the roses, some see the thorns—I love this rabbi, but this is horrible. He reminds us not to beat ourselves up, he mentions "trips with dad." You could be any other son, I could be any other dad. I see Susan put her arm around your mother's shoulder. I hear Bob crying. There's a person I don't know immediately behind me touching my shoulder. The rabbi mentions Nina, as he's putting the folder away, the love of a brother and a sister. He's done. Paul, you didn't live long enough to fill your own eulogy. You were an "oven man," you had a drawing, you liked to travel, you enjoyed the last summer with your mom on the movie set, you took trips with your dad.

The rabbi closes the service, more prayers, announces what will happen the rest of the day.

Years ago, the rabbi had a heart attack and after he recovered, he gave a sermon about lying in the hospital bed and not feeling the need to rush home to tell his wife, his children that he loved them.

"They knew," he said from the same place he's eulogizing you. "They knew."

Did you know? Lying on the floor on Friday afternoon, moments before you died, did you know? Did love matter? Is it possible, in spite of every awful moment you had to endure alone, you knew at that moment?

The rabbi then blesses you, blesses us, and asks the congregation to wait until the immediate family assembles in the auditorium. Walking down the center aisle, I see your stepmom's mother and father, Ellie and Dayne, crying as if you were their son. Dayne held out his arm to touch mine. I crouched by him for a moment. He, too, is in pain. Ann and Tucky, your two preschool teachers, are here—of course they're here—standing together. I see my friend, my publisher, Bill Bernhardt; my friends Mary and Mike Peace; your stepmother's musician friends. None of them knew you. Such sweetness in all of their faces, such tenderness.

Most people in the sanctuary, with the exception of your friends who all left right after the service, are back here with us, eating snacks the Temple has provided. There's love and compassion and smiles and hugs.

Rabbi Fitzerman from the Conservative synagogue, B'nai Emunah, is here, as well. When your stepmother converted to Judaism, he was the one who converted her. It was before she and I married and he probably would have, should have, married us, but they had an argument over some money that Susan thought was owed her—"Rabbi, c'mon, I converted, for Chrissakes!" she screamed at him when he refused her logic—so she didn't ask him to do the service after I told him he could. She hurt him. We hurt him. He told me once he wanted to dance at my wedding. We didn't even invite him. He didn't have to come today, but he's here. He has a son your age.

I pull him aside.

"You didn't have to be here. Susan hurt you—we hurt you. I can't tell you how much this means—"

"Barry, stop it. There is no place else for me to be. This is where I want to be."

Your mom's brothers aren't here. Your mom has to be devastated. How do you not come to support your sister when her oldest son dies?

Before he leaves, John Wooley, a dear friend from *The Tulsa World*, hugs me, and says, "Maybe you don't want to hear this now, but I was just at a Baptist funeral and, let me tell you, your rabbi kicked that pastor's ass when it came to reciting the 23rd Psalm and why that message is so important." Others are coming up, saying goodbye, some while eating cookies.

The place is emptying out.

After the last guest leaves, your mom and Bob grab the flowers and the placard and the 8 x 10 picture of you and the D.A.R.E canister and head toward their car. I grab your ashes, which Scott left with me and which are heavier than I thought they would be, and head to the lobby and sit in one of the Victory chairs. I see your Uncle Ed. Aunt Susan is there, too, and they are sitting on two chairs outside the gift shop, facing me. We just look at one another. I put the urn between my crossed legs with the box leaning away from me. I am looking at you. We're in the blue chair again.

"Is that what I think?" Ed whispers.

"Yes."

"I don't know what …" he says.

"I know."

I don't want to let you go. I don't want to move. I am carrying on a conversation with them, these ashes, with you, with myself, with no one. I hear myself saying words while my son is in an urn in my lap. I feel the box against my legs.

Your mom and Bob have just come back in and said they're

ready to leave. I walk you and them out to their car. Your mom gets in the car and I hand you to her.

"You got him?" I ask.

"Oh, yeah, I got him."

There is a reception at their house. You'll be there in an urn in a box, but this is no wake. We're Jews. We don't yell at the dead. We yell at the living. I walk back inside and see the rabbi leaving. He is carrying a briefcase.

"I think we got it," he says.

I'm not sure. I see him leave out the side door that leads to the back parking lot.

Tell me, Paul: What do you think? Did we get it? Do you even care?

SAME AS YESTERDAY, though in a different part of Tulsa, there are cars parked down the block when I get to your mom's. When I walk inside, I see you on a shelf near the sofa. Your stepmom's brother Blake and his wife Amy are here. He gets up to hug me when he sees me. He is crying, doesn't say anything, doesn't try to. They were at the service, but I didn't see them. And while they dropped Susan's dad at home, her mom is here. You never met any of them. My marriage and life occupy different spaces. I don't know where to sit, my wicker ottoman is taken, so I walk into the kitchen, my old office, the dining room, back into the living room. I am asking people if they want a drink, a snack, anything. I want to keep busy; I want to keep moving. Vern calls me over.

"Sit down and stop it," he says.

"Huh?"

"Stop. I know what you're doing and why, but you can't do this today. It's not what you do. Just sit here," he says again, getting up to give me his chair. "Don't move. Today, people come to you."

Kyle, your old friend from Mario's, comes by. He reminds me that you got him the job there when you two were best friends. A sweet kid, a mess, but always asks about Nina when I see him, always asked about you.

"Can I get up," I ask Vern, "to walk Kyle outside?"

Vern smiles.

"Thanks for being here," I tell Kyle.

"Come by after this is done," he says. "Let me buy you dinner."

"At Mario's?"

"Yeah."

"Perfect. How you doing?" I ask.

"Just come by. I gotta go to work, but I'm telling you something. Paul and I were friends, and I'm here because of that, but this is the last one of these things I'm coming to. That's it, I'm done. No more funerals, no more. These fuckers"—and here he points to some of your friends standing in the hallway who came from the synagogue—"they know what happened and, you know, it doesn't matter. I don't even care anymore. Anyway, come by."

Amy and Blake are leaving, so I walk with them and Susan's mom to their car down the hill on 82nd Street. I help Ellie into the passenger seat and she tells me again, "I could have straightened him out. He's too young for this."

Tense. Present.

ALL THESE CARS, Paul—SUVs, convertibles, trucks—you said you wanted at different times in your life, are on this street. Yours is, too, the white Jeep, still parked in front of the house. I don't know when it will be moved. I think Nina wants it. I had to get your safety deposit key out of it yesterday. The mess inside was comforting; it was all you. As I walk by it now, I look at your Jeep in front of the house—the house I used to own and lived in with my children.

Plural.

Once inside, I see your Aunt Susan talking to Kristin, who's here, again, with the baby in the dining room. I still can't bring myself to go over there, so I walk into the kitchen.

Soon your aunt joins me.

"What?" I ask.

"It's not Paul's baby."

"How can you tell?"

"I picked her up. She needed to be changed."

"What do you mean?"

"Barry, I smelled the baby. It's not a Friedman."

"Listen, we're going to go to Mario's pretty soon ... that pizza place where Paul worked—" At which point your grandfather walks by.

"Who can eat?" he asks, when he overhears the conversation, which makes me laugh.

Your mom can barely keep her eyes open, doesn't really want to go, but, yeah, she'll come. It's a little after eight and the house is almost empty. None of these people are coming back. From now on, this will be an empty house when your mom comes home, filled with just Bob, memories of a death on a Friday, and your ashes on a table near the sofa.

BY THE TIME I get to Mario's, it is past closing time, but Kyle has kept it open for us. It's perfect, where we should be. I park in front. I see you again in the window.

Then I see Kristin and the baby at the far end of the restaurant. Why is she everywhere?

Your mom is there, talking to her. When she comes back, she is shaking her head.

"She says she is waiting for a ride."

"Waiting for a ride?" I ask. "To where?"

"I don't know."

I point to Sam, who agreed to stay and help Kyle, indicating Kristin. I shrug. Sam now has a mohawk that looks like the one you used to have. He started doing drugs I hear.

"Uh, Kristin," he says, "you know we're closing soon."

I can't hear what she says.

"Ask her to join us," your stepmom says to me.

"You ask her. You were just there."

"Come on, Jane," Susan says to her and they walk over.

Your Aunt Susan starts to go, too.

"Wait, wait," I say to her. "What happened this morning? Why were you late? Why were you angry?"

"We got lost. Wayne and Dad were arguing with one another. I screamed at both of them, 'This is not about us, remember that?'"

Kyle brings out pizza, calzone, meatball sandwiches, garlic bread, crumb cake. Nobody's really hungry but we're eating anyway. The weekend is drifting away. I keep staring into the back room where you used to stand. Time is not standing still — it's running backwards. It's late, close to ten, and people who don't have dead children have lives to resume tomorrow.

"Stay as long as you want," Kyle says.

But we should go. Of course he won't take any money.

I walk your mom to the car, say goodbye to Bob, hug Nina.

When I come back inside, I notice Kristin is gone. She never did come over.

"Sam," I ask, "where did she go? When did she go?"

"Some guy came and picked her and the baby up."

SINCE YOUR GREAT-UNCLE and aunt had to take their car back home, I drive your grandfather, Wayne, Hope, and your Aunt Susan to their hotel. Susan, my wife, takes her car, I'm assuming, back to the house. In the hotel lobby, after I hug them all, I remember it was here that I met Roxani, the Peruvian girl I dated. You didn't like her, a thought that makes me smile, as I walk by the exact chair on which she was sitting when I walked up to her and said something that began an exhausting two years together. There isn't a soul in the lobby except me and the desk clerk. The coffee shop and bar are closed.

"Can I help you?" asks the desk clerk.

"I'm just waiting for somebody."

"That's fine," he says. I don't think he believes me.

And why should he? I'm not. I have no particular place to go, even though I have a home and a wife and a life. I'd say I was in a fog, but that's not it. My eyes are heavy, so they won't stay open, but they won't close all the way, either. Once outside, I can see Oral Roberts University, truly ugly, even at night, across the street. There is nobody, nothing but me and a parking lot. Tomorrow, after driving everyone to the airport, I will go by Fitzgerald's, make a payment and then—I don't know what I'll do. I'm supposed to work that comedy club in Providence, Rhode Island, this coming Friday. I should cancel, but maybe I should do it. Would you mind? Your mom has Bob, and Nina will be back at school tomorrow or Wednesday, and Susan and I will just resume being what we were the half hour before you died.

I TAKE the long way home—actually, I take no way home. I'm not even headed there. I crisscross streets, drive through neighborhoods I don't know, double back on roads I just took. I even drive by Mario's, closed now, but enter the parking lot anyway, and park in front of it. This was our Golgotha, Paul.

The bar next door is open.

Pickles.

Remember that Saturday afternoon we had lunch at

Mario's, before you started working there, by the window that looked out where I'm now looking in, and we watched people walk by? We bet who was going in for a drink or coming into Mario's for lunch? Most were going for a drink. You were better at determining who was going where.

I don't want this night to end. This moment is the membrane between worlds, between narratives, between a live Paul and a dead son. I've seen the ashes, I was at the service, I saw the tears and felt the convulsions; still, when the car stops, when I walk into my house, the weekend is over, and this is gone. If I keep driving, it never ends. You're never completely dead.

5. YEAR AND A DAY

I KEEP PUTTING THIS OFF, the end of the elegy. I have been waiting this past year for an epiphany, some bolt-of-lightning understanding, some peace, perhaps, about fathers and sons, about you and me before finishing this.

I heard *Paul Friedman* at the Yahrzeit.

You're past tense now.

A year ago you were still dead.

I'm wrestling with you and you keep changing weight class.

The Wednesday after you died, I called my agent, Kevin, in Vegas and told him not to cancel the Providence gig. Catch a Rising Star, the comedy chain for which I've worked and Kevin booked, sent a nice note and a candy basket. It was snowing when I left Tulsa. When I got to the airport, I was told the flights to Providence from Charlotte, the connecting city, were cancelled, but if I wanted, I could take my chances. I went. Eighteen hours later I was at Charlotte Douglas International Airport, no longer trying to get to Rhode Island, but trying to get home. A crowded, overheated airport in North Carolina with planes neither taking off nor landing is not the worst place to miss your son and wander aimlessly in semi-nausea, better even than lying in bed, waiting for the ceiling to cave in. I walked through terminals, looking at people and wondering who else had dead children and if there was some connection between those who have—a stare, a smirk, like those seen in science fiction movies where only the aliens recognize each other. By the following morning, planes started departing and, after telling a gate agent about you, she took pity on me, put me on a priority list, and got me on a flight back to Tulsa.

"I thought you'd be gone until Monday," Susan said when I called from the airport to tell her I was back in Tulsa and would be home in a few minutes.

"So you're sad I'm coming home?"

"I don't mean it like that. I was just looking forward to being alone. It was a long week."

It was the third week in February. She moved out the first week in July.

IN THE WEEKS and months right after your death, when I thought of you, thought of a story, I wrote it down quickly ... *Paul/Phillies' game ... Curious George ... Ryan and Dr. Pepper ... Chili's ... fat girl/opera ... angels at Which Wich on the backs of used envelopes, electric bills, Panera receipts.* I was not going to not remember. The act of writing about you kept you alive, but on the morning of the second year, February 16, I said *Enough*— literally, in bed that morning, after phone calls from people the previous day who remembered the date, I looked at the ceiling, a ceiling that hadn't changed, hadn't fallen, hadn't sent me a message, and said it.

Enough.

On Father's Day, on my birthday, on your birthday, the moments, some revelatory, some indulgent, seemed to be waiting for me, needing me, needling me, coming in thuds and waves. Once, I saw a volleyball game going on at the University of Tulsa. There were two girls in bikinis, two guys shirtless. I put you in the game and watched you play. On these walks around campus, I would sometimes double over, the pain crippling. No reason it should have happened there, for you didn't play volleyball, didn't go to school there, and I graduated from there more than 30 years ago, but that's where my body convulsed. I'd have to stop, put my hands on my knees and wait for the moment, the cramp, to pass, the wrenching of body and soul and memory to pass. My body had no energy for thought, movement, anything—only grief. Even when my life regained a rhythm, when it was recognizable to me, it wasn't right without you. It was the taste of food when you have the flu. A new club opened in Las Vegas at Planet Hollywood that featured two comedians performing in a show along with bored burlesque dancers. I worked there six or seven times this past year. You would have liked sitting in the back of the room at one of the tall tables, drinking a Yuengling and looking at strippers with names like Dorimar and Brandee. After the show, you and I could have gone to the casino and played Keno with your lucky numbers which were never lucky.

The notes I told you about, the ones I kept writing if just to write and see your name—*Paul drinking virgin daiquiris at the Maxim Hotel in Vegas, Paul buying Nina costume jewelry at the mall when he only had three bucks in his pocket, Paul with braided hair on the beach*—were like filing notarized deeds at the courthouse. Every memory, every thought I wrote down, logged, was now part of the record.

ON THE TUESDAY after you died, Uncle Wayne, Aunt Susan, and your grandfather went home. Your grandfather didn't talk about his cell at the airport, but didn't know what to say, either.

I think of the moments he missed with me and I think of the moments I missed with you. I want your forgiveness. I should forgive him. Maybe, like me, he didn't have it in him to say, do the right thing—or maybe I intimidate him the way you intimidated me. Sons can do that to fathers. When you were two, we were living in Arkansas—Nina wasn't born yet—your grandfather and grandmother came to visit. I had gone out for something and when I came back, he was on the floor and you were standing in your playpen, jumping up and down, smiling and laughing. He looked up at me said, "Paul, show your father what I taught you." My father telling my son to do something for his son. *Father* is a beautiful sound; *son* is a beautiful sound. I was both at that moment. He won't remember that. But he had taught you to pull yourself up by holding on to the mesh of the playpen. I don't ever remember seeing my father on the floor before that. You were holding on, for him, for me.

I ALSO WENT to Fitzgerald's and got official copies of your death certificate. The first copy is free, but you have to pay for additional copies, which you wouldn't think you'd need, but the IRS and Discover and banks and schools won't take a father's word for a dead son, which means I not only had to say the words "My son died" to people in call centers in Mumbai and Davao City, I had to send death certificates to corporate offices. I still have two copies of the certificate in a manila folder that sits next to a large shoebox your mother gave me. In it is an autographed picture of Crystal Bernard from *Wings* when I did *Evening at the Improv* and she was its host and pronounced my name as *Berry*; a Yogi Berra picture from when he was playing ball in the 1960s; one of Carrot Top, who was a friend of mine from the early days of comedy, in which he wrote, "Paul, I'm funnier than your father and Jimmie Walker," who played J.J. on *Good Times* and who you met; every postcard I sent you from my early days of comedy; and a football trophy from the year you played in 9th grade. Bob told me you quit because I told you it was a stupid sport and the coaches were using you because you were big and strong. Your grandfather, when he watches football, says it's a sport played by stupid flesh. You listened to me about that and not about taking methadone and Oxycodone?

A friend planted a rose in your name at Tulsa Rose Garden. I went out to see it and it was good seeing *Paul Friedman* on a plastic stick, even though the flower was dead. Part of me wanted the world to keep grieving, part of me enjoyed the company. All of me wanted to talk about you. I wanted whatever part of you the world saw, even if it was just the part I told them about, even if it was one of drugs and bad parenting, to live on for years. I didn't want you to be forgotten. I didn't want to be forgotten.

I COULD NEVER FIND your safety deposit box. I still have the key, got it from your car, but nobody, not your mom, not Bob, not Nina, knows where I can find the box or the bank that has it.

Maybe it's just a key.

YOUR MOM and I split your ashes. You sit in a metal tin decorated by bad Japanese letters and a poorly drawn mountain range in my office. One of your grandmother's brown gloves sits on top of you, a small wooden turtle leans against you, but I can't remember why or what it signifies.

I HAD lunch with Fred Fleischner one day, an advertising guy I know, who had a son your age who died a year before you from a similar combination of drugs as you. We're not close, Fred and I, but two sons die a year apart, even acquaintances find reasons to have lunch.

We went to Mario's.

"My ex-wife," Fred said, "believes it's my fault, and maybe it is, but as I told her, I have to give our son some of this. It's not all mine. I will beat myself up forever, but Blake has to also be responsible for what happened."

"What do you do with yourself, other than beat yourself up?" I asked.

"I talk to parents, talk to kids about drugs. Go to schools."

"What do you tell them, the parents, I mean? If I went, I don't see how I could give them any hope. Even if I didn't blame myself for Paul, the luck involved —"

"That's it. I tell the parents that by the time your kids are teenagers, it's too late."

"There really are no lessons, are there?"

"No," he said, "there aren't. On Sundays, I go out to his grave and walk around for hours."

"Hours? Why do you do that to yourself? What do you do?"

"I look, stand over his grave, clean up a little around the plot."

"I couldn't do it, Fred."

"What else am I going to do with myself?"

"I couldn't do it," I said again.

"You could. You would. You want to come with me and talk to some kids about drugs?"

"Sure."

He never called. And I never pursued it.

I'M glad you were cremated, Paul, because the thought of seeing you in a grave with a headstone, which would be up now and in place, would be impossible for me. How long after you died did you hang around? Maybe you got tired nobody noticed. I swear to you I tried to find you.

In May, when presumably you were gone for good, I turned

fifty-one, and it hit me we'd never get to that point where I would be twice your age. You needed to live to twenty-seven. A small thing, really, every father and son have a year like that; still, you and I used to make a big deal about it. I was thirty when that happened with my father. I told your grandfather, "This is the only year in our lives where you will be exactly twice my age."

"Okay," he said. "What's your point?"

I CALLED CLAUDIA, my old girlfriend, in Germany. You never met her, either, but I've never loved your mother or Susan as much as I loved her. Had you not been 8, had Nina not been 3, I might have moved to Hamburg. It had been 5 years since we last talked.

"Hey, schnitzel," I said. "I have to tell you about my son."

She knew from the sound of my voice.

"Don't tell me," she said. "Please don't tell me."

"Yeah."

"Sometimes," she said, later in the conversation, "the soul does what the soul wants. And this is what his soul wanted. It wanted to leave. I wish I could have met him, taken him out, gotten him drunk, but, sweetie, you can't expect to win a fight with a soul that wants out. I cry for you later."

WHEN I'D GO into Mario's, I'd see Tim or Kyle or Sam behind the counter. I'd look at them, they'd look at me. There was a dead you between us, connecting us. They treated me extra special. I was your dad.

I would get an occasional call or email from one of your friends, girls mostly, who wanted to tell me how special you were, how strange you were, how sweet, how they loved you. I wrote essays about you for the NPR affiliate in town and I dedicated my March column to you in TulsaPeople. It all seems tinny, laughable even, those gestures. Had I been an architect, I would have designed something. If I had the skills, I would have painted, built, composed, planted something. I'm a writer.

It doesn't seem to be enough, what I do.

TWO MONTHS BEFORE YOU DIED, I was at Panera and met a girl, Valerie, who's a year older than you. She was wearing beige pants and looking for an electrical outlet. Over a loaf of rye bread, she then told me she was "ninety-eight percent" lesbian, which I thought wonderful statistically specific self-analysis, before spilling coffee on herself. Like Susan, Valerie is a musician, so she was nuts. But it was a sweet nuts.

"It's more important," she said to me during another time, right before she once again spilled coffee on herself, "to be a good human being than a good artist." When I got home, I asked Susan if she agreed.

"I'm not so sure about that," she said.

Valerie could have been your best friend. She was mine.

She cried after you died.

"Did you ever teach Paul anything?" she asked the first time we saw each other after you died.

"I don't know. I think so."

"Then he knew he was loved."

"I don't get it."

"That's how we know, people my age. He never would have told you because he might not have known how to articulate it, or maybe he was too proud or stubborn to tell you, but yeah, if you did, he knew." Months later, I told her about your grandfather, how he's never said anything about your death to me, never offered much in the way of support or insight and she said, "How long, how many times are you going to be disappointed by the same thing?"

You would have fallen in love with her that day.

Did I ever teach you anything? And is she right about the connection between love and lessons learned and the permanent link between teacher and student, father and son? On those trips of ours when I first started doing comedy, when I did what was known as the I-70 Tour, when I worked Bushwackers in Manhattan, Kansas on the Monday and Tuesday of the week and Déjà Vu in Columbia, Missouri the rest of it, did you learn anything? Or was just the trip, by itself, enough, the car full of clothes and snacks, the popcorn you ate backstage at both clubs and the Junior Bacon Cheeseburgers from Wendy's we had as soon as we found a franchise open? Was being with your father in the Comedy Car, as you used to call it, enough? What else did you want? What else did you need?

I told Valerie about this book.

"What are you trying to do with it, Ba? What's the point?"

"Great question. I don't know. I think it's an apology."

"Does it feel good, the purging?"

"No."

IN THE FALL semester at OU, Nina moved to an apartment off campus, and on Sundays, I'd drive down from Tulsa and we'd eat healthy in the afternoon and Italian food in the evening. Often, in late afternoon, she'd nap in the bed and I'd nap on the leather sofa I gave her. The more Susan and I limped to the end of our marriage, the more Sundays I drove to Norman to see your sister.

On one trip to Norman, your mom came with me and asked if I'd mind playing the mixtape she wanted to play at your memorial service.

"I have to ask you about Chili's," she said.

"Okay."

"Why did you do that, why did you say that about not

caring why he was mad at you? Don't you know how much that hurt him?"

"Yeah, I know. I knew."

Mostly, though, visiting your sister at school was medicinal. I bought curtain rods and fixed bikes and bought meals for her friends and at the end of the day, driving back to Tulsa, as the sun set, after an enormous hug from Nina, who wouldn't let go, I saw what I should have been with you: a father who doesn't rush fatherhood, a father who loves the sound of his children's voices and logic, and a father who would then be so loved he'd be scolded when he doesn't call upon arriving home safely. I was a better father to Nina than I was to you. On one of her walls, she had one of those cutout frames with different size pictures of just the two of you—not Drew, not your mother, not me. You.

"Do you think Paul would be proud of me?" she asked me one time.

"Yeah, he loved how good you were with the world, how easy you made it seem, how hard you worked."

"Really?"

"Really."

"What do you think he would have said about me going back to school as quickly as I did? You think I should have taken the semester off?"

"I have a feeling your brother would say, 'Don't quit school because I'm dead. That's stupid.'"

She laughed. "Daddy, I heard him say that, too. I did."

You never were jealous of her, were you?

She got a 4.0 ... the semester you died and she returned to school.

Which leads me to what happened that semester. It was the early part of March, a few weeks after you died. It was a beautiful day on campus. I had come down on a Monday. The sun, flowers, the smiles on strangers walking by all conspired to make me forget for a few moments that I had a dead son. As I waited for Nina outside of Dale Hall, waves of students, all preposterously happy and breathtakingly beautiful walked by. Could it really be they were all smiling? Could life really be easier for them to maneuver than it was for you? Could the world have this much beauty, in Oklahoma, on a late Monday morning in March? Did any of them know this might be the best it would ever get and that they would ever be? When Nina emerged from her English class, we walked north, past the armory and the library and the building where we registered in the dead of summer and wound up at Which Wich.

And here's why I'm telling you the story, but I want to tell you first that I don't believe in angels.

A dark-haired girl walked in while Nina and I were waiting to order. She was around your age. She looked at me, looked away, looked back, cocked her head, and then smiled. I smiled back.

She was stunning.

"Dad, forget it," you would have said had you been here, "you're too old for her. She's mine."

Nina whispered, "Do you know her?"

"No. I mean, I don't think so."

"Why is she smiling at you?"

We got our food and walked outside to eat. I looked up and the girl was standing by the table.

"Excuse me, is your name Mr. Friedman?"

"Yeah."

"Did you ever teach at Jenks High School?"

"Fifteen years ago for about three days. I was a substitute."

"You were the coolest teacher I ever had. How's Paul?"

Silence.

I told her.

"Oh, no, I'm sorry. No, no, no! I just wanted to say hi. I remembered you." She put her hand on my shoulder, asked about how and when and why and I told her. She started crying, then leaned down to hug me.

"I'm sorry."

She went back to her table, as she was eating outside, too, to rejoin whom I assumed was her husband and baby.

I don't even remember if she told me her name.

I looked at Nina, who was now looking at the girl and her family, as well.

"That was weird," she said.

"I don't even know her name."

Nina and I saw them preparing to leave, but then the girl made her way over to our table again.

"Sorry to bother you," she said, "but I want to tell you that we all thought you were the coolest guy, the coolest teacher, and when we told Paul, he said, 'Yeah, I know. That's my dad.'" And then she went back to the table, picked up the baby, and the three of them walked west on Boyd Street in front of the university.

"What are the chances of that?" Nina asked. "This restaurant, this day, this hour when you just happen to be down from Tulsa. How does that happen?"

"I don't know, but I have to go talk to her. I'll be right back"

I got up. It couldn't have been more than a minute or two since she had come over that second time. But there was no sign of her. I walked down Boyd. They were nowhere. No man, no baby, no girl. Where did they go? Where was she? I peeked in store windows, went in stores, checked people in cars. I entered Starbucks, crossed Asp Avenue, went all the way to South University.

Nobody.

"Dad, did you find her?" Nina asked when I returned.

"I didn't. She was here, though, right? You saw her? I'm not making this up, right?"

"No." Nina laughed.

I don't believe in angels.

I GAVE A EULOGY.

Susan's father, Dayne, died in September, seven months after you, and his family asked me to speak at the memorial service, even though he had two sons, Hap and Blake, and two daughters, one of whom was my soon-to-be ex-wife. The family I would soon not be in wanted to hear from me at the death of their father.

When I mentioned Blake, the youngest son, in the eulogy, I said, "I don't know what's more difficult ... being a father or being a son."

Thirty minutes before Dayne died, with everyone in the bedroom, Blake crawled in bed with him. A son resting his head on his dad's shoulder as the dad dies.

YOU MUST HAVE BEEN FOUR. You had had a nightmare. You came into our bedroom and asked your mother and me if you could sleep with us. I hesitated at first, but seeing how scared you were, said okay. I turned to your mother for an instant and when I looked back, you were standing there, shaking, at the side of the bed, holding your pillow in front of you. I picked up you and the pillow and put you both next to me. It was the happiest I had ever seen you. It was the best thing I've ever done for you and all I had to do was pick you up. You turned on your side, facing me, and you kept kissing me, thanking me, until you fell asleep, your pillow on both of us. The next morning, with you still next to me and you more awake than I, your mother took a picture of us. You were sitting up, your arms outstretched, making monster faces, my arm around you, my face buried in your neck. I found the picture. I had hair and you had hope.

. . .

BLAKE'S WIFE, Amy, sent me *Beautiful Boy*, a book about a father and son and drugs. The boy lives, I hear. I haven't read it. I'm not going to.

KEN ROGERSON, my friend in comedy for the past three decades, had an awful drug and alcohol problem in the 80's and 90's and it cost him, he told me once, about $250,000, not to mention his career and most of his friends. By the time I met him, he wasn't doing drugs at all and the only alcohol he was drinking was the frozen daiquiris we would have at Paris in Las Vegas, at a bar that looked out to the waterfalls across Las Vegas Boulevard to the Bellagio, when we worked in town.

He called when he heard about you.

"I love you," he said, "but you think you have problems? My Showtime special was cancelled."

It's the kind of thing only a comedian can tell another comedian.

Once, Ken and I were sitting and drinking those daiquiris, eating warm French bread and butter, and looking at the fountains and dancing water at the Bellagio, when I told him I never knew if you ever glanced in my direction and smiled, ever had a moment of pride that we were connected.

"To know you may have had no impact on your son," I said, "that's what stops me. To think I was that insignificant in the first life I created."

"When my dad was dying," he said, "I went to see him. Knew it would be the last time. He asked me about my son, Nick, and I told him that I thought Nick might be doing drugs and that I didn't know what to do and how worried I was. And that's when my father lifted himself, literally, off his deathbed and said, 'Are you kidding me? When you were doing drugs,' he said to me, 'do you know what I went through, how worried I was, what I was thinking? What did you think I was going through?' And that's when I said, 'Dad, I didn't think about you at all.'"

"I'm not proud about that," he added, "but I didn't think about him, so don't think for a minute that Paul thought of you when he was using. It's not like he said, 'My dad's a great guy. I should stop doing this.' Barry, believe me, you never even came up. Not because he didn't love you, but because fathers don't matter to sons at those times. Nobody does. Nothing does. It's only the drugs."

I told Ken's story to my friend Jake, the head of the philosophy department at the University of Tulsa. Jake helped me with *Jacob Fishman's Marriages*, my novel set in a university, that I finished writing a week before you died.

"My God," he said.

"What is it?"

"I can't tell you the last time I even thought about my father, much less what he thought about what I was doing."

I WENT to Italy with your grandfather the summer after you died. He had been there with your grandmother and wanted to go back. He said it was the happiest time of her life. They were on a boat, he told me, in Sorrento, but had somehow gotten seated on opposite ends of the boat. Your grandfather said your grandmother looked at him through all the people and mouthed the words, "Jack, we made it. We really made it."

I don't know why he asked me to join him on this trip.

PAUL, the thing about this guilt that I carry around, is that it crumbles as easily as it takes hold. I didn't do the drugs, I couldn't have stopped you, I tell myself, right before asking myself why I didn't stop you? I wanted to be the biggest presence in your life, to be the kind of father you do think about when you're doing drugs, the kind of father that does make you want to stop. But that can't be all of it. My imperfections can't be why you did drugs and why you died. It can't just be because I fucked up a moment at Chili's. I wonder if the same ego that leads me to think I could have saved your life is the same ego that was the problem?

Susan says you came by the house a few months before you died. You told her about being angry with me, how you wanted to hurt me, embarrass me, and that's why you didn't come to the wedding, that's why you stood me up. She said she liked you.

"I don't blame him anymore, Barry."

"What do you mean?"

"You used him. You made it about you."

"What else did you talk about? What else did he say?"

"He asked if I had any pot."

Perfect.

SUSAN RELEASED A CD THAT YEAR. She dedicated it to her dad and to you.

You were going to be my best man, Paul. People at the wedding were going to see that. You were going to stand next to your sister and me under a Chuppah, the canopy under which Jewish couples marry, and watch me smash the traditional glass to ward off evil spirits. There would be pictures of you and me, hugging, in suits.

My son, my best man.

DEATH KILLS ALL the big dreams and teases me with the small moments, the ones where I found myself saying, "There's a sale on Heinz. Paul would have loved this." I want those moments I never had with you, but I also want back the ones we got right. I didn't know enough wasn't enough, but I thought you might want to be me someday, anyway. When friends of yours, friends of mine, and even angels outside of restaurants in college towns tell me how much you loved me and that I mattered, I'm embarrassed. I snowed them, Paul. I convinced everyone I did all I could for you. I posed. Your mother didn't buy it, your stepmother didn't buy it, your sister didn't buy it.

You didn't buy it.

I threw my shoulders back, yes, but only after you died. I was with Rabbi Fitzerman, the rabbi from the Conservative synagogue, six months after you died.

"Every time I see you," he said, "every time I have seen you since Paul died, you are standing straight, every time I saw you that Sunday and Monday, you put people at ease. You let them grieve. I couldn't do that. Your shoulders were always back."

It worked. But it was performance art.

THE FIRST TIME I said your name on stage, I was in San Antonio, at the club on the river, and I felt my knees buckle.

"So my son, Paul, said, 'I have you, Dad, and I have a stepdad, Bob,' and I said, 'Yes, but no, you really don't. There's just me, your father. You don't need a stepdad, you don't need anyone. Just remember that as long as I'm alive, Bob is just a guy your mom's fucking.'"

It's an awful joke, I know, but I love telling it.

"My son was five when we first talked about sex. Well, actually, that's when he told ME about sex. He said the sex is when a man puts his weenie in a woman's butt. I said, 'No, no, no, that's only if you're really lucky. Even in San Antonio, that's an extra charge.'"

The jokes are almost true, but you ... my son. You're in present tense. The audience laughed, nobody pointed to the stage and said, "But your son's dead. You're a fraud. Your ex-wife is right. Stop using him."

So your mom gave me your Diesel jacket and I look ridiculous in it, but I wear it now almost as much as you did. We were the same size after all. I wore it to Panera the day I met a friend of yours, a girl with piercings and shoulder tattoos, who had recently married. She told me she loved you, but that you had only spent one night together. She said you gave her a massage, which touched her, and then you did an enormous amount of drugs together. She had just quit drinking, she said, so there was something frightening about her, Paul, a look that made me wonder how long before she winds up in jail or is found lying on a floor in her bedroom.

At the off-track betting facility where your stepmom Susan's father used to spend afternoons, I met another a girl who knew you. After Dayne got too weak to make his daily bets, I'd go and make them for him.

"You're Paul's dad and Dayne's son-in-law, right?"

"Yeah."

"Love them both."

Tense again. I didn't know whether she knew about you. I didn't tell her.

As I walked home from the track that afternoon, along the Tulsa Fairgrounds parking lot, I saw a guy, approximately your age, skateboarding. He looked nothing like you, but reminded me of you nonetheless. Like you, he was too old to be on a skateboard in the middle of the afternoon and, more-over, like you, he wasn't very good at it. He couldn't keep his balance, but was determined to complete his flips, turns, hard stops, even as the board flew out from under him each time he'd try a maneuver. I stood, maybe fifty yards away from him, and watched. For a moment I pretended it was you, tried to make it so. He noticed me walk towards him. I waved. He waved back.

"You know, Jane," I told your mother at lunch one day, "sometimes I miss Paul and sometimes I miss my son."

"What do you mean?" she asked.

"Tough to explain, but there's a difference—"

"Yes, Daddy, I know," Nina, who was with us, said. "Sometimes I think about my brother, sometimes I think about Paul."

"You two think too much," your mother said.

You wrote my name.

One day at Mario's, Tim told me about your Myspace page. You had a Myspace page? He wasn't sure what name it was under, so I looked for *Paul, Paulie F, Paul Friedman*, even *Rancid-Rulz*, but it wasn't there, either. I found you under *Pillow Talk Suicide*.

On your bio section, you wrote in the block about idols:

rommel, salvador dali, adam warlock, hank arron, the first porn star, havoc, barry, Miles Davis, Carl, the guys at thrasher mag, Cab Calloway, Hunter S. Tompson, grandpa (both), and every man woman and child that have stood up to destroy the powers that be.

The first porn star?

I'm going to miss you.

I called Officer Kevin Hill, the cop who Bob said was investigating your murder.

"There was nothing." Hill said. "No real investigation. I spoke to that guy Ryan, but he was no help. We see cases like this all the time. I'm sorry."

"This is better. I think. What about the girl at TU, the one who was with the kid who also overdosed the weekend Paul did?"

"We checked. Nothing. He was just another one that day."

So, you weren't murdered and you didn't kill yourself.

What then, Paul?

Taco died.

A week after you died, he went to visit your dealer, who wouldn't give him any drugs because Taco was broke. For some reason, instead of the coke, the dealer told Ryan he could do the white powder on the table in another part of the room for free. So Ryan goes over, snorts it, and then immediately goes into convulsions. The dealer decided not to throw him in the dumpster out back, which, apparently, he did with another kid, and took him instead to a hospital, where it was determined that Ryan had ingested Borax, the cleaner. He survived, somehow. I told the story to your friend, the girl at Panera with the shoulder tattoo, in case she didn't know it, and she said, "Yeah, I know, but don't be too hard on Taco. I doubt he knew it was Borax or that it would hurt him."

"You mean," I said, "there's a difference between someone who knowingly snorts Borax and someone who snorts an unknown white powder that could be Borax?"

"It's all about the high, Barry."

Paul, what happens to a person, what pain is so great in life that makes one decide to take the chance that the stuff he just put in his nose isn't also used to clean toilets and won't kill him? How does a father help his son get through that?

Dad, I never thought about you.

Ryan did die a few months later, anyway, and of course it was drugs. At his funeral, downtown at the Presbyterian Church, Ryan's mom had put up a placard of photos of Ryan in the lobby: Ryan smiling as a toddler, at family picnics, with siblings and family pets. Sound familiar? There was not one photo of the two of you together. Best friends? And then I noticed: like your collage at Temple Israel, the older he got, the more vacant the stare and sad the smile. There were family photos where he looked lost, like a stranger at a reunion. I sat next to your mother, mid sanctuary, and once again, saw your friends lumber in, just as they did at yours, expressionless, preoccupied, bored. Towards the end, the pastor said, "Ryan loved his family and friends, especially Paul, who died earlier this year."

"Omigod!" your mother choked out. "I can't believe he mentioned him."

"Who asked him to?"

Following the service, I saw the pastor.

"That Paul you were talking about," I said, but not as angry as I wanted to, "was mine."

And *Fuck You* for using him as a prop.

"Had I known," he said, "I would have asked you to do the eulogy."

"What?"

"I didn't reach them," he said, motioning to some of your friends in the room. "You might have."

Ryan's mom came up to me in the lobby as people were filing out and said, "I'm glad at least that Paul will be up in heaven to meet Ryan when he gets there."

What is wrong with people?

"Don't take this the wrong way, Becky, but it will be better if he's not there."

"What?"

"The two of them weren't really good together when they were alive. Maybe it's better if they never see each other again."

She stared at me.

"I'm sorry," I said.

But I wasn't. If Ryan loved his family so much—if you did —you wouldn't have allowed your families to go through this. I should be happy, take solace, that while I and your mother and sister have to live, and will forever live, with this hole that traps and mauls us, you and Taco are frolicking in heaven?

I HAD to file your taxes. I know you were expecting more, but you got $182 back from Oklahoma and $890 back from the federal government. I gave a third to your mom, a third to Nina, and paid the balance of your cremation expenses. Before the money could be released, I had to send a copy of your death certificate to the IRS and sign an oath that I was the surviving parent. There was DOD, Date of Death, on each page of the return, 2/15/08 stamped next to it. I had to get used to things like that, things like bills from Oklahoma State University, stating you still owe $9.87 for something, and a note from a collection agency stating you owe $285 to an attorney for something else. You also received a form letter from the Mayor of Tulsa thanking you for registering to vote.

The toxicology report came back in June and you died from *Acute Methadone Intoxication*, but I guess you already know that. The rest of you, though, was strong, unaffected the report said. Item after item, organ after organ, all indicated *Good ... Strong*, according to the report. "Unremarkable," it read over and over. No connotation. It means what it says: no reason for a remark.

Your death was unremarkable.

WE TOOK you to Laureate once, the fancy drug clinic in town. I don't know why we were all together in the same car, your mother, Bob, me, and you, but you agreed to go. Maybe Nina was right when she said you wanted help. The intake nurse, after reviewing the insurance we all had, said, "I don't think we need in-house treatment in this situation."

"Oh, I don't either," said your mom.

Bob agreed. "Not at all."

"Excuse me," I said, "but what exactly would you need for in-house treatment? How many more drugs, how much more denial? We all agree there's a problem. At least we did before we got here."

They all looked at me. They all saw the father—you saw the father—who wanted to institutionalize you.

I found something you wrote on Myspace.

I REALLY DON'T KNOW what to say here, but I guess fuck it, I'll give it a shot. I love drawing and writing even though I'm a terrible speller. I've been working on this one piece of art for about 8 years now (give me a break it's twenty pages). I skateboard even though I'm not as good as I was when I had my girlish figure. I love to travel and sleep. I've been a graphic artist for the last three years and now I work on movies {mostly porn}. I'm a great chef. I went to culinary school but I left because the teachers told me I was too good and was making them look bad. My best dish is peanut butter and jelly sandwiches. I love the rain and that's all folks. bye bye. Don't listen to the next sentence, they're lying to you!

WHAT'S THE NEXT SENTENCE, Paul? Where's the lie? Who says it?

THE JULY BEFORE YOU DIED, on a sweltering Wednesday, you and I went to Sonic for hamburgers and sat outside. The kid waiting on us was huge and struggling. If I had to guess, I'd say he had suffered a stroke or maybe it was some developmental problem because his gait was labored, his gaze was all over the place, and his struggle just to complete a task, picking up a tray, a cup, to get his hands and fingers to cooperate was a chore. It was heart wrenching to watch. He was around 30, wearing a Sonic hat, white pants and a T-shirt, and was completely covered in ketchup, mustard, mayonnaise, grease, dirt, and sweat. You must have seen me looking at him because you said, "Don't worry, Dad, I'm never going to wind up like that."

But that wasn't it, wasn't what I was thinking. I wanted you to be him. He was there. Whatever misery he lives with, he gets up every morning, puts on this preposterous uniform, and finds a way to get to Sonic just to do this, just to walk around in 100-degree weather and clean up Styrofoam and plastic and spoons full of ice cream from metal tables.

YOU'VE BEEN dead more than a year now and I've only dreamed about you twice since last February. In the first, you were with a friend. I couldn't tell who, but it wasn't Ryan. You were standing at a table when I approached. I overheard. No, I didn't overhear. You saw me there. You wanted me to hear it.

"If he were a stricter father," you told this friend, "cared more, did more, didn't spend time chasing girls, I'd be alive right now." You looked at me to make sure I got it.

In the other dream, you were in my living room and you came out from behind an armoire. You had on a plaid shirt. Your skin, eyes, smile all healthy, all remarkable. You were radiant. It is how you would have looked, if there had been no drugs, no divorce, no disappointments. You hugged me around the neck. I could feel the slight stubble of your cheek against mine. I remember feeling the same when I was little and your grandfather hugged me and I felt his beard and his protection. I didn't want to let you go. You weren't letting me. I ran my hands through your hair, your thick lovely blonde hair. I felt your hands on my back. You pulled into me. You wouldn't stop kissing me. And I knew I was dreaming, just as I could hear myself moaning, just as I could feel your stepmom, who inexplicably was lying next to me that morning, trying to wake me up, pushing me slightly.

"Leave me alone," I kept thinking in that half lucid haze, "oh, please, leave me alone."

"Barry ... Barry."

"Stop talking. Let me be. I don't want to wake up, I don't want to wake up."

"Barry, wake-up! Wake-up! Are you okay, honey? What is it?"

Now she was shaking me. I felt her hands on my arms, my back. I couldn't hold on to the dream.

I was awake.

"Honey, you were moaning, screaming," she said. I was on my back. I could feel her open palm on my chest, my heart pounding into it. "You were having a nightmare."

"No. Paul."

I WORKED the Atlantis on Paradise Island in The Bahamas in April, six weeks after you died. I've been going down there for more than 20 years, and it is the time I usually get booked, but you know that. It's when you went with me. I brought Nina with me this time, along with her friend Sara. I also brought you in a prescription bottle. Nina and I agreed that since your best memories were there, we would take you as soon as we could. We would sprinkle you in the ocean, on the beach or maybe near that lifeguard chair. Remember when we'd stay in the villas, back before the drugs got too easy and life got too hard, back when your smile was broad and your eyes didn't droop? That's the Paul I wanted to leave there.

You were something in the old days.

You can research a country's laws on transporting ashes, on the best way to get your dead son out of America, but some things I couldn't bring myself to Google. I transferred some of your ashes from the green tea tin container with the Japanese letters and bad painting of the mountain range because I thought the container might not clear security. I had to make sure I could get you out of the country, so I transferred you to a large plastic Tylenol #3 prescription bottle, removed the label, and put it in my toiletry bag. When I was transferring the ashes, I spilled some on the kitchen counter. Some of you was trapped between the ceramic tiles, so I ran my fingertips over the grout and then my hands over the counter.

I put one palm over the other and pressed you (and probably crumbs, as well) into me.

I poured the rest into the Tylenol 3 bottle.

Immigration left us alone. I could have brought the tin.

THE FIRST NIGHT we got there, Sara, Nina, Richard, the owner of the club, and I went to the Jungle Bar, a few hundred yards from the hotel, where Richard and I usually went after shows, but it was closed, as was the gate to the beach and the ocean. Rather than walk back to the hotel and approach the beach from there, we decided to go into Nassau instead. We would have plenty of time to bring you to the water. Nina put the prescription bottle in her purse and we went first to Flamingos for mojitos, then to Señor Frog's for shots, to Bamboo, for beers, and ultimately to Drop Off for chicken wings and pizza. On the way back to the car, as the sun was coming up and we were walking along Woodes Rogers Walk, a street which runs parallel to the ocean, I asked Nina, "Do you still have your brother?"

"Yeah, I think," she said, looking in her purse.

You were there.

But for a moment, she thought, we thought, she had left you somewhere at one of the bars—a bar in a foreign country, surrounded by drunk girls on spring break. You would have loved that. On the way back to the car, I saw two kids, probably the age you and Nina were the first time you came here, and they were hiding from each other. The boy, the older one, hid behind the corner of a building and when the sister walked by, he grabbed her and started tickling her. She screamed with delight and then they chased each other and disappeared down by the pier, a massive cruise ship behind them and lighting up the walk.

The next night, after the show, we once again went to the Jungle Bar, which was open and packed. After Richard made those at the bar stand, raise their glasses, and toast you, he, Sara, your sister, and I walked through the open gate to the beach and stood at the ocean's edge. Nobody said a word, nobody knew what prayer to say.

"What do we do?" Richard asked.

"Let's look for Vikings," I said.

Nina reached in her purse, handed me the prescription bottle, which I opened, and then poured you into the Atlantic.

"Bye, Paulie," she said.

The ocean took you out with a vengeance.

And then you vanished.

ABOUT THE AUTHOR

 Born in New York, Barry started performing comedy in Tulsa, concluding that while Manhattan was the place to be discovered, Oklahoma had more parking. He has been a regular at clubs in Las Vegas, Reno, NYC, Los Angeles, Atlantic City, on cruise ships, and The Bahamas. Barry's first book, *Road Comic*, chronicled his life on the comedy circuit. In his second book, *Funny You Should Mention It*, Barry continued to explore the cultural zeitgeist of life, love, and humor, but also mused about gun shows, Baptists, old Jews, and Winnie Cooper. Barry has co-hosted "The Politics Blog with Charles P. Pierce" esquire.com; does commentary on *Public Radio Tulsa*; writes a semi-monthly column for *Tulsa Voice*; contributes to *Media Post*; blogs at friedmanoftheplains.com, and reports for *AAPG's Explorer*, an oil and gas journal, even though Barry knows nothing about the oil and exploration business and has been known to hurt himself pumping his own gas.

Made in the USA
Lexington, KY
17 December 2019

58628639R00092